JARROD BARBETTA

POSTMARKED

A Prologue

For Diane

Contents

Preface

Few institutions have wielded as much influence and subtle power in American history as the United States Postal Inspection Service. From its humble beginnings under Benjamin Franklin's watchful eye to its present-day role as a bulwark against modern threats, the Postal Inspection Service has woven itself into the fabric of the nation's communication network, safeguarding the lifeblood of American society—its mail.

Postmarked: A Prologue is more than a collection of historical anecdotes. It is a carefully curated anthology that illuminates some of the extraordinary background of the Plymouth Mail Truck Robbery of 1962. Each story within these pages is also a testament to the bravery, ingenuity, and relentless pursuit of the postal inspectors who have stood as silent sentinels over America's mail system.

These narratives, culled from pivotal historical moments, are more than just tales of crime and punishment. They are the foundational threads that connect past endeavors to the future heist. As you delve into these accounts, you will discover a vital piece of the larger puzzle.

From audacious train robberies to the sophisticated schemes of the early 20th century, these stories provide the essential context for understanding a forthcoming theft that will be explored in the upcoming *Undeliverable: A Tale of a True Caper*. This impending event, centered around the Plymouth robbery, is the most significant chapter in the Service's history.

This prologue sets the stage for the gripping saga that will unfold in the next book. As you finish this volume, hopefully, your curiosity will be sparked, leaving you eager for more. The next installment will not only continue the story but also serve as a dramatic crescendo, seamlessly weaving together the historical threads introduced here.

Welcome to Postmarked: A Prologue

1

Whence They Came

On August 1, 1737, the British Crown's Postmaster General, Alexander Spotswood, appointed Benjamin Franklin as the Postmaster for Philadelphia. In this position, Franklin was responsible for local postal services within the city. Franklin picked up valuable experience managing the infant postal operation, and it was not long before he improved the system's efficiency.

Franklin's innovative approaches and successful management led to more responsibilities. By 1753, Franklin shared a joint position as Postmaster General for the American Colonies with William Hunter. Once again, Franklin extended his influence and implemented improvements throughout the colonial postal system.

This stopped in 1774 when the British dismissed Franklin from his post after his role in revolutionary activities that led to the American Revolution was revealed.

The Continental Congress understood the importance of communication, and, therefore, they established the United

States Postal Service to affirm communications among the colonies. The Congress appointed Franklin the first Postmaster General of the United Colonies on July 26, 1775. The role was new and distinct from his previous position because it was created by the revolutionary government to unify and manage postal operations across all the colonies, removed from British control. This appointment also recognized Franklin's extensive experience and previous success in postal management, which made him the ideal candidate to organize a postal system vital for communication during the Revolution.

However, Franklin buckled under the weight of his newfound duties. On August 7, 1775, Franklin appointed William Goddard as the first surveyor, a kind of 'proto-postal Inspector,' of the newly formed American Postal Service. Goddard's role in regulating and inspecting postal operations laid the foundation for the United States Postal Inspection Service.

On February 20, 1792, Congress passed a comprehensive postal statute (the Postal Act of 1792) that elevated the seriousness of postal crimes. This statute included the imposition of the death penalty for particular offenses, specifically stealing mail. This underscored the gravity with which the government viewed the security of postal communications.

As the 19th century waned, the postal system waxed, and so did the criminal element; therefore, the role of those responsible also needed to adapt to those changes.

On May 1, 1801, the title for those tasked with investigating and regulating the postal system was officially changed from "surveyor" to "Special Agent." The term was used for the first time in Federal Government history; one of the notable figures among the early Special Agents was Noah Webster, who later gained fame for his contribution to American education and lexicography with his dictionary. This is the caliber of individuals who highlight the type of people entrusted with the critical responsibility of protecting the nation's mail.

During the War of 1812, The war disrupted communication lines and seriously threatened the safe delivery of mail, which was crucial for military coordination, government operations, and civilian communication.

A critical duty of the Special Agents during the conflict was to monitor and report on the movements of the British forces. These observations were essential for both military and postal route strategies.

1835, the United States Postal Service created a new investigative branch led by Preston S. Lawbro, who was appointed to the new office of Instructions and Mail Depredations within the Post Office Department on May 6. Under Lawbro's leadership, the office began systematically addressing the postal system's various challenges, mail theft, fraud, and other postal crimes. The newly named 'Special Agents' now operated under a more structured and focused leadership and were sent to different regions in the West to establish new mail services, oversee and regulate postal activities, and protect those routes.

Eighteen years later, the United States was aggressively expanding westward, marshaled by the new opportunities and the unearthing of gold and oil. The United States Post Office Department was presented significant challenges, in which it needed to keep pace in conjunction with the expanding nation.

The Post Office Department made a significant decision to bolster its workforce of Special Agents, increasing their numbers from six to eighteen. This threefold expansion directly addressed the surging demand for trustworthy postal services.

During the arrival of the Civil War in 1861, David B. Parker was appointed as a Special Agent for the Post Office Department and played a key role at this time. Parker supervised the transportation and delivery of mail to Union troops, organizing and securing mail routes that often passed through dangerous areas. He ensured that letters, packages, and official communications reached their intended recipients, despite the risks. After the war, Parker continued his service by helping to rebuild the postal system in Virginia.

By 1873, the Postal Inspection Service had 63 Special Agents organized into 6 divisions, each led by a Special Agent-in-Charge. Later on June 8, 1880, another pivotal moment in the history of the United States Postal Service emerged. Congress enacted a law that redefined the designation of "Special Agent" to "Post Office Inspector." This signified a crucial shift, representing the formalization and professionalization of the Postal Service's investigative division. The change aimed to clarify and specify the duties associated with the role and set the stage for the transformation of the Postal Service's investigative operations.

In 1881, a group of outlaws, led by David Rudabaugh, aka "Dirty Dave," robbed a mail stagecoach near Santa Fe, seizing valuable goods and disrupting the mail service. The newly designated Postal Inspectors, with enhanced authority, launched an intensive investigation to track down the culprits and recover the stolen mail.

The investigation led the Postals across the haggard landscapes of New Mexico, where they interviewed numerous witnesses, gathered evidence, and collaborated with local law enforcement. However, one name kept popping up during the investigation: William H. Bonney, colloquially known as Billy the Kid. But before the Postals could connect Billy the Kid to the robbery, Sheriff Pat Garrett in Fort Sumner, New Mexico, caught up with the outlaw and ended his reign of banditry.

On September 23, 1908, Postal Inspector Charles Fitzgerald investigated a $476 shortage at the local post office in Clinton, Mississippi. During his investigation, he confronted the deputy postmaster, William Sorsby. Sorsby asked Fitzgerald not to report the shortage and promised to make restitution, but Fitzgerald insisted on reporting the embezzlement.

As tensions escalated, Sorsby accompanied Fitzgerald to the railroad station as Fitzgerald was preparing to return to Jackson. There, Sorsby again pleaded with Fitzgerald not to report the crime. When Fitzgerald refused, Sorsby drew a firearm and shot him without warning. Despite being critically wounded, Fitzgerald attempted to pursue Sorsby but ultimately succumbed to his injuries three hours later at the Jackson Sanatorium.

Sorsby was convicted of murder and sentenced to life in prison. However, on January 3, 1919, he escaped from Parchman Penitentiary. Seventeen months later, he was found in Wichita, Kansas. But later enjoyed a pardon by Governor Henry L. Whitfield in September 1925.

Charles Fitzgerald's death marked the first time a Postal Inspector was killed in the line of duty. To this day, the United States Postal Inspection Service has mourned the loss of 15 inspectors.

At the dawn of the 20th century, the United States experienced a significant wave of immigration, with many immigrants, mainly from Italy, planting stakes in urban areas. These Italian communities became targets of criminals known as The Black Hand. The Black Hand was not a single organized group but rather was comprised of various criminals who specialized in the extortion of immigrants through intimidation.

They would send threatening letters adorned with symbols such as black hand-prints, daggers, and skulls, demanding money. Opposition often led to violence, property damage, or even death. The criminals used the postal system to deliver these threats, which prompted the involvement of postal inspectors.

On April 3, 1909, Postal Inspector Frank Oldfield led the investigation into The Black Hand. Oldfield meticulously analyzed the threatening letters, tracked their origins, and identified patterns in their delivery.

Oldfield and his team worked around the clock, monitoring post offices and mail routes and intercepting suspicious letters. On June 15, 1909, A significant breakthrough emerged when the Postals pinched Salvatore Lima for having mailed a threatening letter in Chicago. This arrest led to the identification of other members of The Black Hand.

Through a series of coordinated raids across New York, Chicago, and New Orleans on July 20, 1909, Oldfield and his team, along with local police, arrested 16 individuals in league with The Black Hand. The evidence collected by the postal inspectors played a pivotal role in securing convictions. The members were brought to trial in September, and all 16 were sentenced on October 15, 1909.

The 1920s brought America an economic explosion, and many individuals sought quick and substantial investment returns. Yet, this era of rapid financial growth also provided the fertile soil for fraudulent schemes by conmen. The most notorious was Charles Ponzi.

Ponzi arrived in the U.S. as an Italian immigrant in 1903. By 1919, he had concocted a scheme promising investors lavish returns within a short period. The plan involved arbitraging international postal reply coupons, promising a 50% profit in 45 days. The allure of these high returns attracted thousands of investors. Ponzi quickly expanded his operation in Boston, Massachusetts.

His scheme relied on paying returns to earlier investors using the capital from newer investors rather than the profit earned by legitimate business activities. As more people invested, Ponzi's coffers grew exponentially. By mid-1920, he was juggling millions of dollars from investors who were hungry to get rich quickly.

The Postals became involved when doubts about Ponzi's operations began to surface. On July 26, 1920, Postal Inspector Joseph C. Lawler began sniffing around Ponzi's business affairs.

Lawler and his team analyzed the mechanics of Ponzi's structure. They discovered that the volume of international postal reply coupons required to generate the promised returns far exceeded the total number available worldwide. This revelation indicated that no real profit from actual investments was being produced.

On August 12, 1920, armed with evidence gathered by the Postal Inspection Service, federal authorities in Boston stormed Ponzi's office. The inspection team uncovered that Ponzi owed millions more than he could ever repay. Ponzi was charged with multiple counts of mail fraud. On November 1, 1920, he pleaded guilty and was sentenced to five years in federal prison in Plymouth, Massachusetts. On May 17, 1924, he was cut loose due to 'good behavior.' But that freedom was short-lived. The following year, Ponzi was once again tried and convicted on state larceny charges and was sentenced to an additional seven to nine years in Massachusetts State Prison. Ponzi appealed to overturn the conviction, and it lumbered up to the Supreme Court in 1926, where they slapped down his appeal to overturn his conviction, therefore upholding the lower court's decision.

Again, Ponzi was released in 1934, but his luck had dried up as he was picked up by federal immigration authorities due to his criminal record and status as an Italian immigrant. Ponzi appealed the charges, but his appeal attempts were dead on arrival, and he was deported back to Italy on October 7, 1934. He attempted to live a straight life but had difficulty and soon resorted to his old habits; however, those habits in America were well known in Italy, and he, therefore, found no success there. Ponzi later found work as an English translator, leaning on his fluency in Italian, French, and English.

By 1939 Benito Mussolini's government caught wind of the notorious Ponzi living in Italy. Mussolini appointed the disgraced Ponzi as the manager of the Rio de Janeiro branch of Ala Littoria, Italy's new state-owned airline, and Ponzi was relocated to Brazil to oversee the airline's operations. However, Ponzi's new responsibilities did not last long. The juggernaut of World War II saw the collapse of Ala Littoria, and once again, Ponzi found himself unemployed in a foreign country. He would float between giving lessons in English for little pay and staying in Brazilian poorhouses. In his remaining years, blindness took over, and he suffered a stroke that left him partially paralyzed. Nonetheless, he still bemused anyone listening with his tales of swindle. Ponzi was adrift in poverty, wilting away penniless at the age of 66. Ponzi died on January

18, 1949, at the Hospital São Francisco de Assis of the Federal University of Rio de Janeiro, and was interred in a pauper's grave.

As the 20th century lumbered on, the United States Postal Inspection Service played a pivotal role in numerous historical events. In 1941, the United States Postal Service transferred $9 billion in gold bullion from the New York City Assay Office to Fort Knox, Kentucky. This effort involved 500 rail cars and multiple agencies, ensuring the transfer was completed without incident.

Famously, in 1958, The Postal Inspectors oversaw The Hope Diamond's journey to the Smithsonian Institution. The priceless gem was sent via registered mail from New York to its new home in Washington, D.C., showcasing the United States Postal Serivce's ability to handle high-stakes deliveries with utmost care and without incident.

The United States Postal Inspection Service has safeguarded the nation's security and integrity for over two centuries, marking a legacy of resilience and vigilance. Across its illustrious history, the Inspection service has confronted and conquered many challenges.

The Postal Inspection Service embodies the essence of American ingenuity and determination. Its legacy of excellence and commitment to justice has fortified its reputation as a formidable force in federal law enforcement. The agency continues to uphold the principles of justice and security, preserving the essential services the Postal Service provides. Its storied history and continued vigilance testify to the enduring power of integrity and resilience.

2

The Gentleman Robber

He was the very first Public Enemy Number One in the United States and was born in Brooklyn. Some other folks will say he was born in Manhattan somewhere in August 1887.

His given name was George Chartres. He was no stranger to the inside of prison walls, with Sing Sing being the most notable institution he had spent time in. However, during his time at Auburn Prison, he would undergo a transformation, meeting his mentor and embarking on a path that would lead him to become a successful criminal.

Ivan Dahl von Teler went by the name George "Dutch" Anderson. He was thrust into the world by a wealthy Danish family and had studied at Heidelberg and Uppsala Universities. When the family came to the States, Dutch went to the University of Wisconsin, found it dull, and traded the academic life for the criminal life, leading Dutch to his protege. Dutch took in Chartres. He saw that the boy had the potential to be a big-timer. Dutch taught Chartres his core foundation; good manners and dress diverted attention. No one suspects the well-to-doer.

In 1919, the pair got out on parole and hooked up with an accomplished wheel-man named Charles Loerber. The trio went on a string of successful robberies in the Midwest. They evaded capture by presenting themselves as an oil baron, his business partner, and their chauffeur. In the underbelly, they financed their cushy lifestyle with the criminal vocation of the day—bootlegging and confidence scams.

However, by the time 1921 rolled around, they needed something that paid out more, so they went back to New York and decided to go with something unconventional. And Chartes took on a new persona; that of the sophisticated G. Vincent Colwell who lived in the luxurious Gramercy Park. He took well to the nightlife, so much so that locals began referring to him as "The Count of Gramercy Park." Meanwhile, Chartes and Anderson started casing a mail truck that motored through the Tribeca neighborhood. On the hunch that bonds had to get from point A to point B somehow. For weeks the trio gathered information about the mail truck's route and meticulous schedule.

Loerber's confidence in knocking over a mail truck began to buckle, but Anderson and Chartes assured him that with their combined intellect, the hold-up would be anything but unsuccessful.

The night of October 24, 1921, was crisp and clear. The streets of the Tribeca neighborhood were quiet and still, and a caged mail truck ambled up Broadway. The trio took their positions in the darkness as their prey unknowingly approached.

The gang sprang into action just as the mail trucks reached Leonard Street. Loerber cut off the mail truck at the head, and Dutch cut it off at the back, effectively boxing in the vehicle.

Quickly, Chartes approached the cab with military precision from one side while Anderson came up the other.

Their silver pistols caught the glint of the October moon.

Anderson yanked open the cab door and dragged the driver out from his seat onto the pavement. Chartes rerouted to the back and forced open the back gate. Inside the truck bed were several large and heavy sacks. Chartes quickly transferred the cargo into Loerber's car, wasting no time or effort.

As soon as the sacks were loaded, Chartes and Anderson jumped into the car, and as soon as they sprang into action, they were gone. Picking himself off the ground, the driver clambered back to his truck, but the engine wouldn't turn. He climbed back out, got to the front, and gave the engine a crank, waking it up.

Finally, the driver reached the nearest police station and burst through the doors.

"I've been robbed! Two men with guns…. on Leonard Street… they've stolen sacks of registered mail!" The gasping man sputtered furiously.

But it was all routine for the lieutenant, who carefully opened his logbook and began to make his precise entry.

"I wouldn't feel so bad about it," the lieutenant drawled without looking up. Had you put up a fight, you might not be here now. You should get your superior on the phone."

The driver ambled to a telephone, the excitement still buzzing behind his ear. He called the night superintendent of the Motor Vehicle Service and explained what had happened.

Twenty minutes later, the driver stood before his chief's desk.

"Sit down, Havernack," the chief said laconically, "and give it to me straight."

"Well, I left downtown at about twenty-past nine. I went up Broadway when about a hundred feet off Leonard Street, a pleasure car came up on the right side and cut the road off, then a man jumped on the running board, climbed into the cab—-"

"What this fella look like?" The chief cut in

"Had on a light overcoat and soft hat. Underneath, I think, was a dark suit. Maybe thirty. Shaved and had these bulging blue eyes. couldn't tell much else, except that he had his hand in the coat and had it pressed against me, like he had a gun."

"What about the car; Did you get the number from it?"

"No," the driver shook his head, "I couldn't make it out."

"Alright." the chief nodded and motioned for the driver to continue.

"Another man jumped out of the car onto the running-board. He had a small mustache, looked older than the other, gray, or sandy eyebrows, dark baggy suit and a silver gun in his hand and had thick-rimmed eyeglasses. The man in the cab grabbed the wheel and forced it to the left."

"What about the man behind the wheel of the limousine?"

"Couldn't see anything."

"So you took Leonard?"

"I couldn't do anything else."

"Fine."

"The first man ordered me to turn off the motor and to follow him. We went to the back of the truck and he ordered me to open the lock. Once I did he tore open the grating and began tossing the pouches out into the street."

"Where was the limousine during all this?"

"Parked about twenty feet behind us, blocking the alley we were in off Leonard. Anyways I was ordered back to the cab and a bag got thrown over my head and then my hands were tied to the wheel."

"Your hands were tied to the steering wheel, how'd you get loose?"

"The fella didn't tie the knot too well, I easily slipped it. But by the time I took the bag off no one was around. not a soul. I picked up what was on the street threw the lock back on, cranked up the motor and headed for the nearest police station."

"Did they take anything?"

"Well, I checked on the pouches, compared them with the manifest, and counted five bags missing."

"So you didn't get the registration of the limo... how about the make? Didja get that?"

"Sure, It was a Packard twin-six."

"Alright, get home, get some rest and see Usher in the morning."

"Usher?"

"He's in charge of the investigation."

The following day, the city newspapers ran headlines about the largest heist in U.S. history. The headlines caught the public's imagination.

Postal Inspector Usher and his team began their meticulous work investigating the crime. Usher read over the driver's recollection of the robbery and listened to him tell it after a night's sleep to calm his nerves. After which, Usher dismissed the driver as potentially being in on the job.

It was easy for Usher to deduce that the crooks who knocked over the truck weren't an ordinary lot. They were professionals. The crime scene was clean and free of witnesses other than the driver, which they couldn't avoid unless they knocked him off. Therefore, the fact that he was still alive told Usher that they were not the killing types.

Nonetheless, the task at hand was monumental. Usher deployed undercover agents into the city's underbelly. There, they went into pawnshops, banks, and fences to catch a whiff of the stolen bonds and securities. Over the weeks, informants were cultivated, and every breadcrumb scrutinized.

Shortly, weeks turned into months, but the robbery was the Postal Inspections Services' top priority. A break happened when an undercover postal employee, who had posed as a wealthy bond buyer, got an offer to buy some Argentine Gold Notes.

Jimmy "Slick," a small-time fencer with a black book of significant players in the underworld, sat in a dimly lit speakeasy on New York's Lower East Side. The place buzzed with activity, the air thick with tobacco and the hum of rhubarb.

Across the room is Jack Malone, the alias of an undercover postal agent. He sits at a corner table, nursing a glass of scotch, and scans the room. Malone is here on business. He has spent weeks developing his cover as a wealthy buyer of rare and illicit goods.

Jimmy "Slick" grew a sly grin at the sight of Malone. He got up, took his drink, and slid into a seat across from Jack.

"Malone."

"Jimmy."

"I've got somethin' special you might like. Real high-end stuff."

"That right?"

"Sure. Argentine gold notes."

"Interesting. Where from?"

"The source. Straight from."

Malone leaned in with a feigning interest. "Sounds intriguing. Who's the seller?"

Jimmy's eyes flicked around the room and back to Malone. He took a sip of his brandy and spoke in a low voice;

"Guy name G. Vincent Colwell. Top shelf guy, like yourself, but moves around in fancy circles."

Malone's heard the name Colwell. During briefings, it came up a few times back at the Post Office, but nothing immediately popped up when he was checked on. Colwell seemed too polished of a guy to be hanging around grimy alleyways. Malone stifled his excitement.

"Set up a meeting. I'd like to see if they're any good."

A few days later, Jack arrived outside No. 12 Gramercy Park. He looked at the slip of paper he got from Slick again. It was the right place. The address oozed with opulence. The doorman escorted Malone to an apartment on the upper floor. The door opened at once; behind it was an immaculately dressed man with radiating sophistication.

"Mr. Malone, I presume?" Please, do come in."

Malone's eyes were met with an apartment, a perfect testament to wealth and taste. Fine art hung on the walls, and expensive furniture filled the room.

"Quite the place you've got here, Mr. Colwell."

Colwell smiled, a calculated gesture to disarm. "Yes, well, thank you. Shall we get down to business?"

Colwell produced an attache case, gently set it on a cherry-wood table, and opened it to reveal the soft glint of gold notes, preciously sitting. Malone examined them. This was it—the breakthrough that was needed.

"Impressive. How much are we talking?"

"A fair price is all I'm looking for, considering the rarity and value of the notes, of course."

Malone nodded appreciatively.

"Well, I'll need some time to gather the funds from my banking institution. Say we meet again tomorrow night," Malone looked around again, "Same place?" Then smiled.

Colwell's smile returned as he plucked a fleck of tobacco out of his mouth. Colwell agreed, "That sounds fine."

Malone returned to the Post Office, his excitement barely contained. Fresh from a pivotal meeting, he was eager to share the latest developments. Bursting into Usher's office, he wasted no time.

"Do you have the serial numbers from the heist?" he asked, his voice charged with anticipation.

Usher looked up from his paperwork, raising an eyebrow. "Of course, why?"

With a grin, Malone pulled out a slip of paper and waved it. "Let's see if we've got a match."

Usher motioned for Malone to join him at his desk, clearing the way. Together, they pored over sheets of serial numbers, meticulously cross-referencing them with Malone's note. The room grew thick with tension as they worked through the list.

Finally.

Usher leaned back in his chair, letting out a slow breath. He glanced at Malone's eager expression. "So, Colwell has the goods," he said, more to himself than anyone else. He paused, considering the implications. "Can you get us another meeting?"

Malone's grin widened. "Already did. We're set to meet at the same place on Wednesday."

Usher nodded, a look of determination settling on his face. "Good. This time, we need to make sure everything is airtight. No mistakes."

Malone agreed, his excitement now tempered with resolve. "I'll go over the plan again and ensure all bases are covered. Colwell won't know what hit him."

As Malone left Usher's office, the gravity of the situation settled in. They were getting closer to breaking the case wide open, and every detail mattered. The investigation was far from over, but they had a solid lead. The clock was ticking. Wednesday could not come soon enough.

Wednesday evening, Malone sat at a polished mahogany table in the lavish apartment at 12 Gramercy Park. He methodically thumbed through the gilt-edged bonds, each one a testament to Colwell's illicit gains. Across the room, Colwell, brimming with confidence, began to pour himself a celebratory drink. The crystal decanter caught the light, casting shimmering patterns across the opulent furnishings.

The tranquility was abruptly shattered as the door was violently kicked open. The sound echoed through the grand room, and in an instant, a cadre of Postal Inspectors and New York police officers stormed in, their badges glinting under the ornate chandelier.

Colwell's face twisted in shock and outrage. "What's the meaning of this?" he shouted, thrusting his hands into the air, the drink forgotten.

Usher emerged from the crowd with an air of unshakable authority. "Never mind that now, Colwell. You're coming with us," he said, calm but firm. He moved with purpose, the heavy thud of his footsteps marking the solemnity of the moment.

As Usher approached, he produced a pair of handcuffs and clamped them onto Colwell's wrists with a decisive *snap*. Colwell's protests faded, and his bravado buckled in the face of the overwhelming force of law.

With Colwell being led away from the museum he called home. The officers began to methodically search the apartment. The air was thick with tension and the inevitability of justice being served. Malone stood back, watching as the scene unfolded, the culmination of their meticulous work coming to fruition.

Following Colwell's arrest, the atmosphere at the Post Office was one of cautious optimism. The investigators knew they might have finally caught a significant Leonard Street Mail Robbery player. However, the full extent of Colwell had yet to be uncovered.

Back in the interrogation room, Colwell sat across from Usher, calm and collected. Despite the circumstances, he exuded an air of confidence.

"I think you've made a horrid mistake," Colwell sneered. "What ever it is that you think I've done, I haven't."

Usher leaned forward, his gaze unwavering. "We already have more than enough, Colwell. We know you're involved in something big, and we have the evidence to prove it."

Colwell's eyes flickered with amusement, "Those bonds? They came to me legitimately. As I've said, you're barking up the wrong tree." The weight of the situation began to settle in, though his pride kept him from showing any sign of concern.

Meanwhile, Malone and the rest of the team worked tirelessly to piece together the information they had gathered. Among the evidence collected from Colwell's opulent apartment was a ledger filled with transactions and connections to various financial institutions. However, it raised more questions than answers.

Malone laid out the documents on a large table. "We need to cross-reference these entries with known associates and previous cases. There's something more here that we're not seeing."

As they meticulously combed through the ledger, a pattern began to emerge. Several entries were linked to a vaguely familiar alias: Gerald Chapman. The deeper they delved, the clearer it became that Colwell was a false identity used to cover a more notorious past.

The Postal inspectors tracked down this Chapman on the hunch that he may be behind the curtain pulling the strings. An unexpected break came as they continued to grope around in the city's dark corners. Charles Loerber came forward and wanted a confidential meeting with the postal inspectors. Usher and Malone, sensing the potential for a significant breakthrough, agreed immediately.

Shortly, in a dimly lit back room of a nondescript building, the informant, a wiry man with darting eyes, sat across from Usher and Malone. His voice was low, almost a whisper, as he leaned forward.

"Word has it yous pinched Colwell," he began, glancing around nervously. "Well, I've got information you might be interested in."

Usher glanced at Malone, both leaning in closer. "What do you have for us?" Usher asked, his tone steady but urgent.

Loerber swallowed a deep breath. "He ain't who he says he is."

"What, he's got an alias?" Malone said.

"No, Colwell is the alias."

"How's that?" Usher broke in.

"That fella's real name is Gerald Chapman."

Malone's eyes widened in shock. "Gerald Chapman?"

Loerber confirmed with a nod. "He's been living a double life, hiding behind the Colwell alias. I'm tellin' yous, he's a master of deception, always one step ahead."

"How can we be sure?" Usher asked, his voice betraying the weight of the moment.

Loerber explained that he'd been Chapman and Anderson's driver since the Midwest days and now fears for his safety. Eager to secure a deal, Loerber had decided it was better to get ahead of the pair and turn on them before they could turn on him.

Loerber then pressed his back against the booth and pulled a small key from his jacket, sliding it across the table. "This is the key to a shack just outside of New York. Inside, you'll find a bread box and in that, yous'll find everything that prove Chapman and Colwell are the same person and more of the loot. It's all there."

Usher took the key, examining it closely. "A bread box?"

Loerber nodded. "Chapman thought it was the safest place to keep his secrets. You'll find everything you need there."

"This changes everything," Usher murmured, a mix of disbelief and determination in his eyes.

"Well, I think I gave you dicks enough," Loerber said. "I can't keep lookin' over my shoulder. This ought to help me out."

Usher and Malone exchanged a glance. They knew they had leverage now, but they also recognized the genuine fear in Loerber's eyes.

"We'll see what we can do," Usher said. "But you need to kick around awhile. We might need more from you later."

Loerber nodded gratefully before slipping out into the night. Usher and Malone remained, the weight of the new information pressing down on them.

The team gathered at the Post Office around a large table covered with maps, documents, and evidence culled from the bread box. Usher stood at the head, his demeanor calm but focused.

Malone, scanning the documents. "Chapman and Anderson have been working together for years. They're like two sides of the same coin."

The team reviewed the evidence meticulously. The ledger in Chapman's apartment contained several entries suggesting transactions and meetings with Anderson. They knew Anderson was critical to Chapman's operations, often handling the more dangerous and intricate aspects of their heists. It was clear that he had to have been the gunman on the mail truck running board.

A clearer picture began forming as they cross-referenced the ledger entries with Anderson's known activities. The financial records indicated a series of payments and transfers between Chapman and Anderson, often disguised through various fronts and aliases.

Malone found crucial evidence. "Look at this," he said, pointing to a series of transactions. "These payments were made to an account we know is controlled by Dutch Anderson. It's not just money; there are notes about meeting places and logistics."

Usher leaned in, studying the entries. "That's it alright. We need to move on this information."

With the new evidence, the team began to map out Anderson's known hideouts and contacts. They planned coordinated raids to capture Anderson and gather further evidence to solidify their case against Chapman.

The day of the raids arrived, and the team moved swiftly. Usher and Malone led separate units to the various locations identified in their investigation. Each area was carefully chosen based on the intelligence they had gathered.

Malone's unit targeted a safe house in a quiet neighborhood. As they approached, the tension was palpable. They broke down the door and swept through the building, finding Anderson in a back room, surrounded by incriminating evidence. He went easy without incident, though his expression showed he knew the game was up.

Meanwhile, Usher's unit raided another location, uncovering more documents and communications that linked Anderson to Chapman. The evidence was overwhelming.

Back at the Post Office, the team consolidated the evidence. The documents and testimonies from the raids produced a comprehensive picture of the petty criminal enterprise run by Chapman and Anderson. The connection between the two was undeniable, yet their downfall was targeting the U.S. Mail, so investigators were confident they could bring the total weight of the law against the pair.

The investigators knew they had a significant breakthrough with Chapman now in custody. However, Chapman's cunning nature was not to be underestimated. Held in a secure facility, Chapman began to plan his escape meticulously.

One evening, during a routine exercise period, Chapman took advantage of a momentary lapse in supervision. He bribed a guard with promises of wealth in exchange for assistance. Motivated by greed, the guard smuggled a wire for Chapman to use.

Using the wire, Chapman managed to pick the lock on a maintenance door. He slipped through the door unnoticed and went to the facility's outer perimeter.

Outside the facility, he found a hidden cache of tools and a change of clothes he had managed to stash earlier. Disguised as a maintenance worker, he calmly walked through the gates, blending in with the end-of-day shift changes.

A car waited nearby, driven by an associate who had remained under the radar. Chapman slipped into the car, and they sped away into the darkness.

The alarm was raised soon after. The postal inspectors were immediately notified, and a massive manhunt ensued. While Chapman's escape was severe, they knew he would not remain idle.

After Chapman escaped prison, he fled to Hartford, Connecticut, where he sought refuge with Walter Shean, a scapegrace of a wealthy family in Massachusetts. Shean provided Chapman with a hideout and the means to stay out of sight. However, funds were running low, and soon Chapman became Desperate for cash and increasingly reckless; Chapman plotted out the robbery of the Davidson & Leventhal Department Store in New Britain, Connecticut.

On the night of October 12, 1924, a hostler from a nearby stable spotted some suspicious activity at the store and telephoned the police. Five officers responded to the call, including 18-year veteran Patrolman James Skelly of the New Britain Police Department.

When the officers arrived at the scene, they spread to cover the various exits of the store. Patrolmen Atwater and Skelly moved along the alley behind the store and came through a rear door. They confronted Chapman, who was coming down the rear stairway as they went inside. Chapman, realizing his escape was blocked, quickly drew his gun and opened fire.

Officer Skelly was hit multiple times in the abdomen. Despite his injuries, he managed to identify Chapman as his shooter before being transported to New Britain General Hospital, where he succumbed to his wounds a few hours later.

In the chaos of the shootout, Chapman managed to escape, but Walter Shean was apprehended nearby by Officer Malona. Shean quickly turned informant to avoid the death penalty in connection with Skelly's murder. He identified his accomplice as Gerald Chapman, confirming the suspicions of law enforcement.

Chapman again went into hiding, this time in Muncie, Indiana, where he stayed with a farmer named Ben Hance. Suspicious of his lodger's behavior, Hance tipped off the police, leading to Chapman's arrest on January 18, 1925.

Chapman was extradited to Connecticut to stand trial for the murder of Officer James Skelly; the trial was a media sensation, with significant evidence and testimonies from Walter Shean, who had assisted Chapman, and Ben Hance, who had unknowingly harbored a criminal fugitive. Chapman's attorney argued that his client couldn't be hung until he first fully served out his federal sentencing stemming from the mail robbery, that being 25 years. However, the courts thought differently, and the jury found Chapman guilty. He was sentenced to death by hanging.

After weeks of the sensational trial and newspapers fawning

over Chapman's prison poetry and philosophies, on April 6, 1926, Gerald Chapman was executed, marking the end of his notorious criminal career.

Meanwhile, shortly after Chapman escaped prison on March 27, 1923, Anderson pulled the same stunt, escaping from Atlanta Federal Prison six months later on December 30, 1923.

Anderson laid low for a while, but that changed when he saw that Chapman had been picked up in Muncie, Indiana. Anderson sought retribution.

On August 11, 1925, Anderson and another man named Charles "One Arm" Wolfe forced a car belonging to the Hance off the road. Anderson emerged from the instigating vehicle, approached Hance's car, and shot both Ben and his wife.

Later, another motorist came up and found the idling vehicle and assumed they needed help, approached the car, The Samaritan discovered the horror behind the wheel and immediately alerted the police.

Police were able to trace the shooting back to Anderson from testimonies, and an APB went out seeking the individuals.

Following the murders, Anderson continued with his criminal endeavors, which included counterfeiting. This eventually led to a shootout with police on October 31, 1925, in Muskegon, Michigan.

Anderson and Detective Charles Hammond died in the firefight. "One Arm" would later answer for his part in the murder of the Hances.

3

Train 272

Train 272 departed North Station and headed toward Salisbury in the early morning of July 29, 1926. Bill Jordan, the baggage master, went through the passenger cars to the smoking car at the back, intending to enjoy a cigarette and log the cargo report while travelers boarded. As Jordan sat down, lighting his cigarette with his trench lighter, he heard another clicking sound. He then felt the barrel of a gun pressed against his head.

"Make it fast," a voice commanded from behind the pistol. Jordan raised his hands and stood up, slowly turning to face his assailant. A grim-faced man with a scar along his nose glared back at him. The gunman pressed the muzzle into Jordan's chest, forcing him back toward the door of the car.

Another man, younger, entered the car with the brakeman, held at gunpoint. The back door was flung open, and the two trainmen were shoved out as the train negotiated a curve.

After disposing the trainmen, the bandits produced a knife and tore open the canvas bags. Eventually, they discovered three leather pouches. The bandits tossed the pouches out the same door they had thrown the trainmen. They leaped from the train moments later, leaving the smoking car empty.

Meanwhile, two other men watched in a nearby sedan as three mail sacks dropped from the moving train. Once the train had passed, the driver engaged the engine, and they calmly picked up the sacks and placed them in the vehicle. The sedan then drove to Cronin's Crossing, where two men were dusting themselves off. The men hurriedly climbed into the sedan, which sped off, bumping along the potholed road.

Elsewhere, Jordan and the break man scrambled to Salisbury Station to telegraph the incident. The telegram reached the desk of Postmaster General Park D. Colvin, prompting an immediate investigation. *How did these crooks know about the money?* The only logical explanation had to be it was an inside job.

While city police began cordoning off Amesbury and Salisbury, postal inspectors questioned a succession of employees involved in the transportation. Truck driver John Concannon, who took the sacks from the Postal Annex to North Station, had no information. The baggage man at North Station, known as "Brown," also had no information. However, an exciting development emerged when they questioned the baggage master of the victim train.

The following day, July 30, an employee of the Walton Amusement Agency came forward to the Boston Post Office and explained to lead investigator Carl Nelson that he had been carjacked the morning of the robbery. His story went like this: The employee had driven down from New Hampshire and pulled over by Cronin's Crossing for a bit of shut-eye. At 4 a.m., a rap came at the driver's window. It woke him, and he saw another car idling across the street with three men standing by. The man at his window calmly and casually asked what valuables he had on him. The employee answered honestly— only five quarters—and without a word, the man returned to the group by the car, and they disappeared.

In hindsight, Nelson should have paid more attention to the story rather than rationalizing that the bandits wouldn't have stooped to petty crime when a major haul was on their horizon within hours. Nonetheless, the Postal Inspectors ordered a total roundup of all known criminals in the surrounding area on the hunch that someone had the breadcrumbs that would lead them to the culprits.

Meanwhile, back in Boston, the Railroad Company, the Federal Reserve, and the Postal Inspectors denied any wrong-doing regarding the lack of mail protection. These denials became more pronounced after publicizing that such mail transportation was common and typically carried out on branch lines throughout New England without armed guards.

Another development occurred on August 1: five bootleggers were arrested in Belfast, Maine. They were quickly connected to the case because two of the men hailed from New York, which was a point of interest as the license plate spotted on the alleged getaway car was a New York plate. Acting on a hunch, the Postals suspected these could be the same bandits who pulled off a New York Mail Truck robbery of April 6, 1926, and may have pulled the Massachusetts job, too. However, the five suspects were quickly cut loose from the investigation as they were found not to be involved with either heist.

The Postals continued their investigation with little success. However, they noticed that some of the stolen banknotes began appearing at various banks around Newburyport. By August 26, the Postals had issued a directive to all banks and businesses in the city to monitor incoming bills for any matching the stolen currency closely. The total stolen amount was $65,000, which included $40,000 in $10 bills (with $6,000 in new gold certificates), $17,000 in $5 bills (with $3,000 in new Federal Reserve Bank of Boston notes), $4,000 in $2 bills (with $2,000 in new United States Mint notes), and $4,000 in $1 bills (with $200 in new silver certificates).

By Autumn of 1926, the United States faced an unsettling crisis. A series of daring mail robberies had left the public anxious and the postal service in disarray. The most audacious of these crimes occurred on October 14 in Elizabeth, New Jersey, where James "Killer" Cunniffe and his gang hijacked a mail truck, killing the driver and escaping with $161,000. The brutality and scale of this heist echoed through the nation and demanded an immediate, decisive response.

President Calvin Coolidge could not ignore the mounting crisis. On October 19, 1926, after consulting with his advisors, he issued an executive order to use the U.S. Marine Corps's might to help the postal service. This decision was not without precedent; it recalled when President Warren G. Harding first dispatched Marines to combat a similar wave of mail thefts back in 1921.

The deployment began swiftly, and by October 21, the first detachments of Marines were stationed along the most vulnerable mail routes. Over 1,850 Marines were strategically positioned at crucial railway hubs and postal facilities, with an additional 650 on reserve, - Including the 16th Company 5th Regiment at Boston - These Marines, armed with trench guns,

M1911 pistols, and M1903 Springfield rifles, stood as sentinels against the chaos threatening the nation's mail.

Secretary of the Navy Curtis D. Wilbur's orders were unequivocal: "When our men go as guards over the mail, that mail must be delivered, or there must be a Marine dead at the post of duty." This uncompromising directive underscored the seriousness of their mission and the government's resolve to protect its communications lifeline.

Major General Smedley Butler, a national hero and one of the most decorated Marines in U.S. history, was at the forefront of this operation. Butler, known for his fearless leadership and tactical acumen, carefully oversaw the deployment. His presence added a layer of prestige and assurance to the mission.

As October gave way to November, the impact of the Marines' presence became palpable. Reports flooded in nationwide, praising the sudden cessation of mail robberies. Newspapers like The New York Times featured stories of armed Marines riding alongside mail trucks and trains, and the public began feeling renewed security.

By November 15, the Postmaster General reported to President Coolidge that mail operations were proceeding without incident. The Marines' disciplined presence allowed the Postals to focus their efforts toward investigative and preventative measures, bolstering the overall security of the postal system. With their steadfast dedication, the Marines had become the guardians of the nation's mail.

Meanwhile, the Postals intensified their surveillance of Biddle & Smart, Inc. employees following a tip-off from baggage master Jordan. By mid-November, they had compiled detailed records of employees who had either been terminated or had quit. Over time, they routinely checked in on these former employees, focusing mainly on those who had left voluntarily. Another point of interest for the Postals was employees who exhibited signs of sudden, unexplained wealth.

The persistence paid off. Towards the end of November, the Postals uncovered their first significant clue: one employee had recently purchased a new car in cash and a plot of land to build a home. Not only that, but the employee's son, who had coincidentally quit his job shortly after July 30, also bought a new car. But the anomalies did not end there.

The employee's daughter had abruptly left town with her young child, abandoning her husband. Rumor had it she had eloped with another man—another former Biddle & Smart employee. These individuals were placed under close surveillance.

Complications arose when the father of this family found himself in a jam over in Concord, having to pay a $600 fine for liquor possession. He managed to cover $500 out-of-pocket and sent his unemployed son back to Nashua to fetch the remaining bit. A Sergeant who was involved in the liquor case was poised to raid the Nashua home in search of more contraband, but his chief ordered him to drop the matter without further explanation. Frustrated, the Sergeant later confided in a friend, unaware that this friend was, in fact, an undercover Postal Inspector who did not want to spoil the mail robbery's investigation and alerted the Sergeant's commander of his frustrations in order to temper the heat so that they can continue to gather intelligence and evidence about this family's potential involvement.

January 27, 1927, it was a cloudy and drizzly day in Galveston, Texas. Postal Inspector John Hunt had been in town for just under a week. His investigation had led him from New Hampshire to Galveston following a tip from Postal Inspector H.M. Hageney. The tip was based on a description of the bandits involved in a Massachusetts mail robbery, which had been dispatched to all postal inspectors nationwide. Hageney noted that a newcomer in Galveston bore a striking resemblance to one of the suspects described, particularly a man with a distinctive scar running down his nose.

Hunt also had a photograph of a girl from Nashua who was alleged to be associated with the suspect. Using this photograph, Hunt connected the dots and traced the suspect to a small fruit and confectionery shop at 708 Tremont Street. Acting swiftly, Hunt organized a raid on the shop. The operation was quick and efficient, resulting in the arrest of two men, John Boyd and John Maleyeff, without any resistance. Inspectors discovered 111 $5 Federal Reserve Bank bills and 90 $10 Gold Certificates inside the shop, all brand new. Oddly, the arresting officers found in Boyd's coat was found a Philadelphia municipal court subpoena for a person named Stephen Susan.

Satisfied that he had his man, Hunt sent a telegram to Chief Postal Inspector Colvin. During the subsequent interrogation, Detectives Frank Anoilo, E.E. Goode, and Fred Forde uncovered that the two arrested men were not just associates but brothers. John Boyd's real name appeared to be Fred Maleyeff, but when asked about the subpoena, he plainly confessed that he was indeed Stephen Susan. Both men were held on $40,000 bond by U.S. Commissioner Brantley Harris as they awaited extradition to Massachusetts.

Back in Massachusetts, Chief Postal Inspector Colvin signaled to move in on 133 Ash Street, Nashua, NH. Just before 4:30 p.m., a team of 20 men, including Postal Inspectors and local Nashua police, led by Postal Inspector John Breslin, Chief of Police Irving S. Goodwin, and U.S. Marshal Chertian, approached the Ash Street residence, which was under renovation.

The six carpenters working on the house paused to watch as the law enforcement officers cordoned off the area. Before Breslin could knock, the front door swung open to reveal a young woman. Breslin lifted his lapel, revealing his badge, prompting her to ask, "How did you get wise to it?" before fainting. Inside the home, the officers found a man recovering in bed from an apparent gun-cleaning accident and identified him as the woman's brother.

Additionally, John Andrews and his son Michael were found in the house and did not put up a fight. A thorough search of the house yielded about $1,200 in small, fresh bills. Elsewhere, around 5:00 p.m., Detective Ed McCarthy of the Nashua Police Department informed Colvin that he had apprehended another suspect, William Hovonisian, on Brooks Street. Chief Goodwin instructed the Sergeant not to put the suspects in the same holding cell or block out of fear that the Andrews would craft an alibi for themselves. Nonetheless, Goodwin's instructions were ignored or, at best, misunderstood.

The Postals case fell into place shortly after that. William Hovonisian confessed to being part of the robbery as the sedan driver. However, he claimed he didn't enjoy the spoils of the robbery as he had only been paid $5 for his work as the wheel-man. Michael Andrews was the next to crumble under interrogation. He detailed the whole heist from top to bottom, and the confession sealed the men's fate: he and Boyd were the robbers, and his father and "The Greasy Pelican," the name he used for Hovonisian, were in the getaway car. He explained that he and "John the Russian," as he called Boyd, learned of the payroll being transported on the B & M on Thursdays.

As for Stephen Susan (that is, John Boyd, Fred Maleyeff), he was found to have been wanted for killing his wife, Minnie Susan, in her mother's Philadelphia home on January 15, 1925. Minnie filed a request for separation. A dispute about the separation with his wife led her to request a subsequent court order to shield her and their three young children from Stephen. Enraged by the court order, Susan allegedly killed his wife and fled.

Last spring, Susan, using the names Fred Maleyeff and John Boyd, obtained a job at a shoe factory in Amesbury, Massachusetts. He reportedly studied the movements of the bank messenger who transported the factory payroll from Boston. When brought back to Boston, Susan admitted his true identity but did not mention any warrants for the murder of his wife. The court order and a photograph of him shown to Minnie's mother and sister were crucial in his identification. There was some dickering among litigators about whether or not Susan would stand trial for the murder first or for his hand in the robbery. Nonetheless, The trial of Susan in Boston was postponed due to the illness of his counsel.

Meanwhile, evidence against him and his accomplices in the Salisbury robbery continued to mount. Bill Jordan, the baggage man on the train, testified that Boyd held him up at gunpoint. Jordan described the holdup in detail, highlighting Boyd's involvement.

William Hovenetian, the government's chief witness in the

robbery case, also testified extensively, noting that he got involved because he had been told that the trip was for acquiring liquor. He, too, identified Boyd and the Andrews men as the perpetrators, detailing their actions on the robbery day. Other witnesses, including break-man Harry F. Babcock and station-master Irving A. French, provided testimonies corroborating the robbery. They identified the defendants and described the events leading to the holdup.

Defense counsel surprised the court by painting a picture that William Jordan was the real mastermind behind the robbery. They claimed Jordan orchestrated the entire event and that John Andrews had no involvement. The defense argued that Jordan's life was never in jeopardy and that he was complicit in the crime. But the defense's allegations against Jordan were met with skepticism, and the prosecution emphasized the credibility of their witnesses, so the Jordan matter was abandoned.

After an hour and a half of extensive deliberation, the jury found the three defendants guilty, bringing closure to the first major mail robbery in Massachusetts.

4

The Robbery That Went Too Right

The Postal Station inside the F.B. Holand General Store in Barre Plains, Massachusetts, was robbed by an 18-year-old. It did not take authorities long to arrest Victor Lawrence Magoon. He was convicted on November 5th, 1914, and ended up doing a year and a day in jail for that crime. However, when he got out, it was clear that he was not rehabilitated. Magoon got picked up again for another petty theft and ended up before a lenient court in Worcester County. The Judge considered Magoon's age and granted him a pass on one condition: that he join the Army. Not being a fool, Magoon took up the opportunity, and off he went.

Victor found his beginnings as a soldier enlisted for duty at the Mexican border in 1916 with the 3rd Infantry, Regular Army. From there, Magoon was transferred to the 26th Infantry of the 1st Division, Company "B," an assembly of young men who were being prepared to potentially enter into the swirling storm overseas. And sure enough, in early 1917, America entered into the fray of the World War. Once across the Atlantic, Company B took on further training in

Gondrecourt, France, with the American Expeditionary Forces, that continued shaping the men for the crucible ahead.

Soon, Magoon and Company B faced the bleak realities of trench warfare. In the northeastern city of Toul, France, the men laid under a heavy blanket of hardship in the trenches and were psychologically rattled by the nerve-burning toll of waiting for the subsequent explosion, the next friend to be torn apart by the relentless hale of enemy artillery and moments of haunting silence that brings a foreboding feeling of imminent destruction that makes the sudden eruptions of violence all the more terrifying.

After Magoon's deployment in Toul, Company B moved to Picardy in March of 1918, directly into the ferocity of the German spring offensive, known as The Kaiserschlacht. This was Germany's strategic yet desperate attempt to break through the Allied lines before reinforcements, particularly the full deployment of American forces, could arrive and potentially turn the tide of the war. Company B, including Magoon, later played a pivotal role in the Battle of Cantigny, the first major American offensive in the heart of Germany's advances. For their gallantry in the face of the enemy, members of Company B, such as Magoon, were recognized with the Silver Star for their bravery during this critical moment of the war.

The thick summer heat of 1918 smothered the charred landscape of northeastern France as the Aisne-Marne Offense unfolded. The goal was to drive the German forces from the Marne River Valley. Again, with the American Expeditionary Forces, Magoon bore the brunt of that determined push. The Allied Forces then launched a surprise attack. The conflict was fierce and dizzying under an unrelenting sun. The Allies sought to break through Germany's lines, but in doing so, they faced its sinister defense deployed on the Western Front; poison gas.

The use of poison gas introduced a new layer of horror to the theater of war. In one skirmish, Magoon was caught in the gassing attack and suffered immediate and terrifying effects, despite protective measures. Symptoms of suffocation and horrific burns were compounded by the clipped pelting of German bullets, marking the beginning of Magoon's grueling journey of recovery. The severity of his condition necessitated his removal from the front lines and into an arduous period of convalescence. The wounds he sustained underscored the personal sacrifices made by himself and others in the earth-rattling conflict.

Magoon spent time in various hospitals in France and later in New Jersey. He was discharged with a 75 percent disability rating from the Rahway Hospital in New Jersey and left the Army behind in October 1919.

Despite his heroics on the Western Front, Victor Magoon returned to a life of petty crime after leaving the service. Throughout the 1920s, Magoon was picked up for these petty crimes. Sometime in 1922, Magoon took employment with the Post Office in Lowell, Massachusetts, under the tenure of Postmaster Xavier Delisle. By 1924, Magoon was caught red-handed by postal inspectors.

At that time, the Post Office had a "Pilot House," a small private room elevated above the mail room floor where Postal Inspectors would occasionally, and unannounced, watch over the handling of mail by the employees. Magoon knew about these Pilot Houses and, in this case, attempted to circumvent the watching eyes by plugging up the peepholes. However, unbeknownst to him, he was being watched at that very moment. The incident ended up with Magoon getting suspended. Shortly after that, bureaucrats in Washington touted Magoon's heroics in the First World War. The political heat was turned up under Delisle, forcing him to reinstate Magoon's employment.

By 1931, Magoon was still employed by the Lowell Post Office. He is now the treasurer on the board of directors and watches over money shipments. He had befriended 22-year-old Louis A. Skaff. A mail truck driver.

One night over drinks, the pair hatched a plot to take a piece of some valuable registered mail shipments, nothing large enough to cause alarm but just enough to be quietly comfortable. And so The question became, when? Magoon told Skafff he'd let him know when the time was right. Weeks passed, and soon Magoon learned that a bundle was being put together to join in on a ride that would make a pickup from the Post Office on the Woodsville, New Hampshire, to Boston Railway. Mail car number 24 under the consignment of the Union-Old National Bank of Lowell is to be delivered to the Federal Reserve Bank of Boston on December 31st.

The time had arrived. Magoon rolled out the outgoing mail from the Post Office onto the loading dock where Skaff was waiting, which was another ordinary night for the two. Skaff loaded the mail sacks onto the truck except for two bags, which were slipped into the brush near the dock. Skaff entered the truck, headed to the train station, and loaded Train Car 24. After that, he waited at the station for the North Bound trail to pick up cargo and return to the Lawrence Post Office.

On Saturday afternoon, January 2nd, Skaff arrived at 147 Moody Street in Lowell and met Magoon at the City Hall Garage. There, Magoon took out a rental from the Drive-Yourself-Auto Company, which was coincidentally located there. Magoon took off with the mailbags in the back seat on a single trip of roughly 23 miles.

On Monday morning, Postmaster X.A. Delisle was going through the weekend receipts. He noticed that the 12/31 delivery receipt was missing. But he wasn't alarmed. After all, it was the holiday weekend. Perhaps the Reserve hasn't processed that night's delivery yet.

Nonetheless, Delisle dispatched a 'tracer' to find out about it. The Tracer went to the Boston post office and spoke with William E. Hurley to obtain the receipt, but when they looked over everything, it was quickly discovered that there was no receipt. Hurley then immediately got Postal Inspector Park D. Clovis involved.

By the time the newspaper's morning edition hit the streets, it was already known that money had been stolen from the mail train. Seeking an interview for the newspaper's next edition, men inquired about the matter to see if it was true. The Postals, while not wanting to discuss the case, held a press conference with bank president John F. Sawyer, and although they conceded that there had indeed been a theft, the banks would not suffer any losses. Delisle believed that his office would have the matter all wrapped up in a matter of days as he's got his top men, James J. Breslin, Thomas P. Cronin, and Byron S. Hall, working the case.

After a night of heavy rainfall, the Postals announced on January 7th a reward of $10,000 for anyone finding anything related to the December 31st robbery and another reward of $10,000 for the total recovery of the loot stolen.

Moody Wiktrowicz, a young farmhand, comes upon two registered mailbags with their contents pilfered, laid splayed open at the foot of a steep embankment beside Andover Road near the North Tewksbury tow line. Not knowing about the reward announcement, Moody notified the Post office of his discovery and received an excellent day's pay. Not too far away, a lineman for the New England Power Company, Albert L. Deggs, discovers mail sacks buried in a by-path just off Hood Farm Road in Tewksbury. Deggs calls the post office at the top.

Meanwhile, the three sturdy Postal Inspectors toiled away on the case. They canvassed the surrounding area where Moody and Deggs had discovered the bags. The three-man operation worked far into the night, questioning potential witnesses with an itching feeling that the caper had been the handy work of insiders.

Working with a hunch that the culprits may have rented a car to avoid suspicion, The first rental agency they checked out was the "Drive-Yourself System" in Lowell at 147 Moody Street, where they discovered that there had been a car taken out on January 2nd. That afternoon, the Postals and Police Captain David Petrie held a press conference. But Captain Petrie was quickly pulled away around 6:30 p.m. Petrie went into a behind-closed-doors meeting with Postmaster Delisle on the second floor of the Post Office Building.

At 8:45 p.m., he broke during a second interview with Louis Skaff. He made a complete confession in which he implicated Magoon in the theft. Meanwhile, down the hall, Magoon also broke while being interviewed by Captain Petrie. At that point, Magoon agreed to escort Petrie, Breslin, Cronin, Hall, and Police chauffeur James Lannon to Haggett's Pond in Andover in the direction of Shawsheen Village to where he had initially stashed the loot, the registered locks, and the iron mail lock on the outside of the registered sacks.

Then Magoon took them to his home, where a jar containing the rest of the loot had been unearthed in the basement of his rooming house at 6 Olive Street, Lowell. A total recovery of the stolen loot. $99,100 from the Tewksbury woodlot and $900 from the basement canning jar.

Upon arriving at the Lowell Police Office, Magoon threw himself to the floor as if a bomb had gone off. Quickly, a doctor was consulted and managed to calm Magoon down. Magoon told the doctor that he was 23 years old and in the Army, which was curious. Back at the Post Office Building, at 10:30 p.m., Skaff's mother and wife demanded to see Skaff and were quickly denied entry. Immediately, Captain Petrie got word about the Skaff women and jumped into the police car and sped off.

By 1 a.m. on January 9th, a sizable crowd of newspapermen had jammed the Post Office corridors, pregnant with excitement and anticipation.

Something was about to pop.

At 3:30 p.m., Victor Lawrence Magoon, 36, and Louis Skaff are arraigned before United States Commissioner Richard B. Walsh in the commissioner's hearing room in the Middlesex County courthouse in Boston, under section 1623 of the Postal Laws and Regulations, among other things. Bail was set for $10,000 for both Magoon and Skaff. Skaff's family and the Lowell Syrian community pitched in to help cover for him. Magoon could not cover his bail, so Deputy Marshal James Mahan took him into custody and sent him to the East Cambridge Jail. While being entered into the system by Mahan, Magoon again broke down and began acting strangely. On the edge of tears, he told Mahan that he was 23 and employed as a corporal of the first squad. Magoon was given two days of psychological evaluation.

On January 11th, the newspapers interviewed Etta Farrar, Magoon's sister, and she recounts that she had been unable to see her brother due to his "condition." However, her father believes that Magoon had sufficiently recovered from his "mental affliction" and provided for bail. Generally, the family was shocked that he had been involved in the robbery as he had been receiving $50 per day as a veteran of World War I and that he had known that if he needed any money, his family would have seen to it. There were more revelations from the interview.

It was discovered that Magoon had a grocery list of priors, which at one point had gotten him fired from the Post Office but had his job reinstated due to political pressure. The Postal Inspectors declined to speak with newspapermen about Magoon's past. Meanwhile, Representative Edith Rogers, who was said to have been the one turning up the heat on the Post Office to reinstate Magoon's employment, told reporters that she couldn't recall if she had any opinion of Magoon at that time and stood on her current statement that no one should be employed by the Government with a criminal record.

On January 13th, Lorel N. Morgan, Deputy First Assistant Postmaster General, issued the following statement in response to Senator David I. Walsh's demands for an explanation of Magoon's reinstatement:

"This employee worked faithfully for the Government for many years before his past misdeeds came to the attention of his immediate superior. The Post office authorities then took up the case with the Civil Service Commission. Both groups came to the conclusion that Magoon's good work in the postal service and his unusually fine war record warranted his being given a [second] chance. His suspension did not follow any new wrongdoing, but merely the discovery by the Lowell Postmaster of Magoon's previous history. We decided the man's apparently new attitude justified his being allowed to continue in the service."

Morgan went on to say that the situation did come up in 1930 and that the department made another intensive look into the matter only to find that Magoon's "slip-ups" had happened when he was a young man and that his war record spoke louder than his past actions.

Nonetheless, Magoon's mental state was still questioned. After much dickering about the matter, Magoon was once again evaluated. On February 4th, the Psychopathic Hospital Authorities informed U.S. District Attorney Haven Parker that Magoon was sane and would be returned to the custody of the U.S. Marshals by the afternoon.

On March 1st, Parker reported the Hospital's findings to Judge James A. Lowell. On one hand, Parker believes that Magoon is a responsible person and can take responsibility for his crimes. Conversely, Magoon's attorney, Leo Doherty, believes that the evidence that he had collected, statements of friends who believe Magoon is insane, and a family history of being inmates at insane hospitals warranted yet another review of his client's mental state. The following day, Judge Lowell ordered that Magoon be examined again by alienists. Dr. Winfred Overholser of the State Department of Mental Diseases did the examination this time.

The trial was held on April 29th, 1932, before Federal Judge Letts. Initially, Magoon entered a plea of not guilty on the six charges against him, but he ended up changing that plea. Magoon was sentenced to four years for the first count to be served in Atlanta, and for the other five accounts, he received probation.

As for Skaff, who was charged with helping Magoon's embezzlement, pleaded guilty and was given a sentence of one year and a day in Worcester Jail and five years probation.

5

Wendelschaefer

1: Odd Street

It was another routine day for Herbert Reid. He woke up, dressed, washed his face, and left for work. He punched his time card and got his orders from the desk in the post office garage. He turned the ignition to the assigned mail truck and motored off half a mile toward the railroad station. It was early morning, January 23rd, 1935, and the weather bit briskly and hard.

At seventeen past eight, the train from Boston lurched into the station. Its trailer doors slid open, and two men appeared in the opening. Reid backed up his truck to the trailer, threw open his doors, and welcomed the mail pouches on consignment from the Federal Reserve Bank of Boston to the B.M.C. Durfee Trust Company for payrolls in the city mills. Ten minutes later, the job was finished. Reid dropped back behind the truck's wheel and left the rail station, aiming the truck's motor for the heart of Fall River.

Reid rounded the corner and ended up on North Main Street. The mail truck puttered along the quiet and desolate street. Suddenly, two men jumped onto the vehicle's running boards, one on either side. The bandit at the driver's window jammed his pistol through the opening and stuffed it tightly against Reid's ribs.

"Odd Street!" the bandit barked, "Take it, Odd Street, next over!" he barked again, pushing the gun barrel further against Reid's rib cage.

Not willing to risk his life over a direction, Reid made the turn. "Take it to the curb, nice n' slow," the bandit snarled. The mail truck ambled down Odd Street and came to a slow halt. The bandits jumped off, and Reid's door was thrown open. "Come on, come on, git out! I'm gonna drive this heap," the bandit said, pulling Reid by the sleeve, causing him to tumble out.

The bandit from the passenger side came around the truck and trained his pistol on their captive. The driver-side bandit took from his topcoat a dark handkerchief and affixed it around Reid's head, hoodwinking him. Reid was taken by the two bandits, arm-in-arm, and hurried into a waiting automobile. The door flung open, and he was thrown into its tonneau. Reid's feet clumsily searched for footing. On their way, they found what felt like two machine guns on the floor. The car door was slammed shut behind him, sounding like explosions in his eardrums.

The car jerked forward, bouncing off the curb with a *thunk*. The drive felt like an eternity to Reid. He could only speculate on the destination. Was he being driven to his grave? Was he going to make it out of this jam? All of these thoughts flooded his mind like a dark kaleidoscope. Reid fought back, attempting to focus on something else. Figuring it would be best to shift his attention to the car's direction, its turns, and the spaces between them. But he had no luck. He had lost his bearings while concentrating on his survival. Soon, he felt the car slowing down and coming to a stop. His heart began to race; where was he?

The door opened, and an invisible hand clutched Reid's arm and yanked him out onto his side into sloshing snow. The invisible hand searched Reid's pockets frantically and pulled a set of keys from his left pocket. The roughhousing had pushed the blindfold up, and Reid watched the feet of the bandit traipsing their way to the back of the mail truck. Reid counted at least five sets of shoes. A pair of shoes stopped and pivoted back, a voice called out, and another pair ran towards Reid. He pinched his face closed as the bandit drew him up from the ground and slammed his back against the side of the car.

"Don't look at me!" the man shouted, startling his victim as he fumbled with the blindfold. The man gritted his teeth and said, "Don't you look at me, or I'll let you have it." Reid was then spun around and slammed again into the car. His hands were jerked behind his back. Adhesive tape leaving its spool sounded and was quickly tightened around his wrists. There was more commotion, and Reid was thrown into the snow again.

The adhesive tape bound his legs next as the commotion continued. Wet shoes sloshed back and forth. Reid began to prop himself up, but the invisible hand returned and shoved Reid's face back into the grimy snow.

"Stay down!" a voice shouted. It was all chaos in darkness. Reid's gut would catch a soggy kick every few moments, a reminder that he was not alone. Helpless and shrouded, Reid did not want to think again about what was potentially coming next. He did his best to listen for anything that might be helpful to the police later or that might be some sort of murderous cue. But he heard nothing, just indistinct mumbling, heavy breathing, and what he suspected to be looting.

Moments later, the chaos subsided. The bandits got into an idling car. At this moment, Reid knew he had to seize his chance. He pushed himself up and braced for another round of slugging, but nothing came, so Reid broke free of his bonds and tore off his blindfold.

Herbert Reid was alone with a mail truck on a snowy, lonely wooded road littered with undelivered mail scattering with the breeze.

Adrenaline flushed through Reid's veins as his cold, wet fingers struggled to bite into the bindings around his ankles. Once free, he stumbled, propped himself against the truck, and found that the keys were gone. He gathered what little strength he had left and lobbed himself down the soggy street. Reid needed to get help. As he ran, his legs felt like a bag of bricks.

Reid made it to the Swansea-Fall River highway and began frantically waving at passing motorists to no avail. Yet he did not give up; He had to get help. Just then, a car stopped, and the driver leaned over to the passenger door and rolled it down, "You in trouble?" the driver asked.

The stranger's car quickly took to the curb at the Fall River Police Department. Reid leaped from the vehicle and burst in, sopping, frozen, beaten, exasperated, and desperate.

"I've been robbed!" he shouted and began to collapse before he was caught by two officers just as his escort entered from outside behind him.

2: Off Brayton Road Lane

Herbert Reid, a thirty-year employee of the United States Post Office Department, went over his harrowing morning with officers and investigators. They also questioned the Good Samaritan, Russell Ainsworth, who gave Reid the lift to the station. The Northern Police station then flashed word about the robbery over teletype to surrounding cities and town stations for good measure. The notice was simple: *Keep Your Eyes Peeled For Five Men Armed In a Nondescript Auto.*

Prowl cars and detectives were dispatched to the site of the hijacking. Combing over the whole street, they encountered a bent registration plate in a dirty snow bank. The tag was called in and came up as a green sedan registered to a Pawtucket man, Peter Dubois. However, the law did not want to put all its eggs in that one basket, as there was no telling if that plate had not been ripped off earlier.

Connecting the dots of where Reid had been abandoned in Swansea to where he had been picked up on Odd Street, the detectives determined that from Odd Street, the sedan and mail truck had gone over the Brightman Street Bridge and then down Providence Road. There, they hooked a left and lumbered on for three miles out of the city, picking up Brayton Road Lane and then rolling onto a narrow road.

The established route was dispatched across the teletype, buzzing to the Taunton and Pawtucket Police departments. A short time later, more pieces of the puzzle tumbled into place. Massachusetts State Police discovered an abandoned sedan along the Fall River-Providence Highway. Its registration was checked and found to have been sold to James Javino of New York City in 1927.

3: The Nassonville Fork

A Black sedan idles in wait at the Smithfield-North Smithfield town line in early February. The street is still fresh with light snow. The driver flips on the windshield wipers, clearing away damp snow from his sight of the blooming golden sky. Meanwhile, an old junker drifts by the black sedan and, in another moment, a U.S. Mail Truck. The black sedan driver shifts in his seat and eases out into the main road onward behind the mail truck, keeping a respectable distance along Farnum Pike.

Rounding a curve, the mail truck approaches a junkyard. The black sedan gasses up, closing the gap between it and the mail truck. In another lane, a car passes by. The black sedan shifts into the opposite lane; the coast is clear. The driver speeds up, neck-to-neck with the mail truck. Howard Stevens, the truck driver, glances out of the driver-side window and spots the black sedan. He glances back to the road ahead, not believing the sight. He snaps another look.

The man in the passenger seat of the black sedan cautiously steps out onto its running board; using the door as a prop against his body, he draws a pistol and levels its barrel. The cold, wet wind whips the gunman's orange-clothed face. "Pull it over!" he shouts. "Pull—It—Over!"

Reacting quickly, Stevens wrenches the steering wheel as hard as possible towards the sedan, smashing violently against it. Its driver, unable to control the impact, weaves, and the masked gunman spills onto the roadway running below. Stevens stomps on the gas, giving it speed it has not felt in a long time, if at all. Stevens looks in the rear-view mirror as he makes his getaway. Behind him, the black sedan stops to scoop up its fallen confederate.

With space between them, Stevens had another surprise for the orange-masked crooks. The road ahead split into a fork; Stevens aimed the truck toward Woonsocket. The black sedan, back on its feet, regained momentum on its target. At just the right time, Stevens cut the wheel, and the truck blustered across the median just before the jersey barriers and careened hard down the Nassonville Fork. The black sedan had no chance and, like a bullet, flew in the wrong direction toward Woonsocket.

Stevens arrived shortly at the Lincoln State Police headquarters. He explained what had happened to the troopers there, and once again, word went out on a wire to all police stations in the immediate area. Soon, cordon posts were propped up in Providence, Woonsocket, Lincoln, and more. Cars moving in the area were stopped and inspected. City hospitals and local doctors were called to report on any recently injured men.

Later that day, Postmaster Edward F. Carroll told an eager press that he would not elaborate on the exact figure Stevens was hauling. Though assured them that had the crooks been successful, they would not have had much of a payday.

4: Wendelschaefer

On a Thursday night in April, Andino (Tony) Merola, a numbers pool operator, one-time suspect in a 1930 attempted state prison break, and recently a self-confessed participant in the Big Chief Market Robbery in June last, was secretly picked up in an automobile out of the watchful eye of federal and postal investigators. April 25th would be the last time anyone would see Merola alive. Merola was found in the back of his own car just off the bank of Lake Pearl in nearby Wrentham, with a bullet lodged in his skull and another stuck in his side for good measure. Cryptically written in the caked dust of the car was "*Freddie St. Louis*," which baffled investigators.

Chief of the New England Postal Inspection Division, John J. Breslin, approached the podium before a corral of press reporters. "There has been a robbery of a mail truck at Fall River." Breslin told the crowd, "The bandits kidnapped the driver, bound him, and looted the truck. The Postal division is prepared to pay a $10,000 reward—$2,000 per bandit—for information that leads to the capture and conviction of these criminals. These men will face—if convicted—a 25-year stay in the federal prison." Allowing the flashbulbs of cameramen and reporters to digest the announcement. Breslin stepped off, and lead Postal Inspector Benjamin Hatfield took over the podium.

"Good afternoon. I am Benjamin Hatfield, postal inspector of the Providence, Rhode Island district. After a check with the Federal Reserve in Boston and other officials, we can confirm the amount stolen to be $129,000," Hatfield told the press. "There are a few clews that are being closely followed. We've got a team of inspectors in Fall River and Providence investigating the caper."

At the outset, it was pretty apparent that any intelligence about the consignment delivery had to have been limited to employees of the Federal Reserve, selected postal employees at Fall River, and payroll employees at B.M.C. Durfee Trust Co. It was evident that someone along that line had betrayed a trust and either gave it over to the robbers freely or by fee. This was not a random robbery, as the bandits took specific sacks, leaving behind postcards, utility bills, and love letters. These men had to have known how to tell the difference between a registered mail sack and an ordinary one. And it could not be discounted that these men had clearly known or had been attentive to the truck's route from the station to the post office.

Elsewhere, at 444 Central Park West, New York, a man and his wife began to gather what they could as soon as possible after a desperate telephone conversation.

As the investigation progressed, Investigators continued to piece together information, identifying connections and building a profile of the gang involved. Merola's involvement became increasingly evident. Records showed frequent communications between Merola and Carl Rettich, a suspected criminal mastermind. Financial records indicated that Merola had been laundering money through various businesses, some directly tied to Rettich. Furthermore, surveillance and informants confirmed that Merola often visited the Wendelschaefer Mansion, known as Rettich's stronghold.

Merola had been in debt to Rettich, having borrowed significant sums to cover his gambling losses and fund his illegal operations. Despite this, Merola had refused to give Rettich a cut of the profits from the Fall River job, believing he could handle Rettich's pressure. Rettich saw Merola's actions as a betrayal that needed to be punished to maintain his authority and prevent others from defying him.

The break that Investigators needed came from Merola. Dead men apparently do tell tales. Top federal agents made the call in Rhode Island, and five simultaneous raids swiftly kicked off. One was at a lodging house where Merola held a room at 390 Weybosset Street. Another was at Merola's mother's house at 127 Ring Street, another at the home of Joseph Fisher, 104 Radcliffe Avenue, Providence, and finally, at 41 Burnett Street,

Johnston.

On the shoreline of Narragansett Bay, at Warwick Neck, sat comfortably a 25-room house known as The Wendelschaefer. Built in 1901 by Felix Wendelschaefer, the manager of the Providence Opera Company. Early in the morning, the peaceful abode was violated by a law enforcement team under the command of Post Office Inspector Benjamin Hatfield, William Goucher, U.S. Marshal, and J. Howard McGrath, U.S. Attorney. Law enforcement diligently and systematically, like a surgeon's scalpel, scoured the house, finding weapons stashed away in strategic points; presumably, in the event of a raid, the occupants could take up arms and have a shootout. A lot of good that did them now. Finding the house empty, officials descended into the cellar, which was a massive enclosure. An officer searching found a lever that appeared to control some electric apparatus. Taking a chance, the officer yanked the lever, which caused a section of the floor to spring open.

A sub-cellar.

Cautiously, the officials centered flashlight beams at the mouth of the sub-cellar. With no indication of anything roaring up the stairs within the opening, the agents relaxed and entered the cavity.

Inside, agents came across a cache of weapons: .30 caliber machine guns equipped with silencers. One of them was jury-rigged to be affixed to a boat. Also found were .45-caliber automatic pistols, .45-caliber sawed-offs, thousands of rounds of ammunition, bulletproof vests, blackjacks, and so on. All in all, the quaint house was actually a criminal armory, sufficient enough to arm a platoon of criminals.

While the Wendelschaefer did not yield any bodies, the wide raid by law enforcement was not a total bust. Providence Police and federal agents were able to pick up fifteen people at the four other raid sites. One of these fifteen was particularly interesting: Ira Steele and Emil Rettich. Ira is Carl Rettich's brother-in-law and Carl's father, Emil. Steele is also the Wendelschaefer caretaker and was taken to the United States Marshal's office in Providence and was grilled extensively throughout the night. Though he refused to give anything up, authorities provided Steele's family, his wife and two children, who had also been caught up in the toil, a measure of protection in the event of an assassination attempt. They charged Ira with conspiracy concerning the Fall River Mail Robbery to show Ira they were not fooling around.

Despite that, Steele only offered up crumbs to the investigators and remained uncooperative. Having no choice left, inspectors placed his wife under arrest for conspiracy as well.

That was when the trap door opened.

Under immense pressure and the threat of his family being harmed, Ira finally broke down and revealed everything. He detailed how Merola had been skimming money off the top of their operations and had fallen deeply in debt to Rettich. When Merola refused to pay his dues and tried to cut Rettich out of the Fall River job, Rettich decided to make an example out of him. Ira disclosed the gang's inner workings, including financial operations, hideouts, and plans. He provided vital information that linked Merola's murder directly to Rettich's orders, which confirmed the investigators' suspicions and solidified the case against Rettich and his associates.

5: Warwick Point

Chief Postal Inspector John J. Breslin stood bleary-eyed at the podium before the press. A tsunami of questions washed over him. Some were predicated on rumors, while others were close enough to the truth to make Breslin curious about an internal leak. He motioned for the crowd to quiet down. Once they complied, he spoke:

"Today, the $129,800 Mail Truck Robbery at Fall River… is solved." Breslin paused, letting the weight of his words settle over the room. He then launched into the details of the investigation, revealing how the break was made. It all began with his inquiry into the automobile used in the robbery, leading him to Herbert H. Hornstein, who used the alias "Frederick Powers," who had registered the car at a bogus address and was traced to the West Coast. There Postal Inspectors extradited him to the East Coast to face additional charges.

"Meanwhile," Breslin continued, "we received a tip that Merola's killer was a Worcester thug, formerly of a Providence outfit. This individual was in town the same day Merola disappeared, allegedly to Worcester itself. Unidentified sources indicated that Reittch had come to put the squeeze on Merola. It turned out that Merola had refused to give Worcester a cut of the Fall River profits, despite being in debt to them."

The room buzzed with the implications of this revelation. Breslin then shifted to another crucial discovery. "Authorities at the Internal Revenue Service office uncovered that Merola had been footing the bill for Carl Rettich's income taxes in 1933 and '34. This discovery was made when the bureau checked everyone implicated in the Rettich trials, as well as those who assisted Rettich in converting the peaceful mansion in Warwick into the criminal stronghold it had become."

Breslin detailed how Steele and Hornstein, under pressure, had finally cracked, providing the crucial information needed to solve the case. "Their confessions opened the floodgates, linking the Fall River Mail Robbery to a rash of other unsolved crimes. They even provided clues to the kidnapping and potential murder of Daniel Walsh, which stemmed from a botched $40,000 payment in a Boston hotel."

He paused, allowing the press to absorb the gravity of the interconnected crimes. The room fell silent, hanging on his every word. "This investigation has been a testament to the relentless dedication and coordination of local, state, and federal law enforcement agencies. The successful resolution of this case is a significant victory against organized crime."

Breslin's voice grew stronger, filled with resolve. "These criminals believed they could operate with impunity, but today, they face justice. The Postal Inspection Service will continue to work tirelessly to protect our nation's mail and bring criminals to justice."

6

"I'm Not Going to Make It"

Bill jammed his foot onto the brake pedal and threw the machine into drive. The others flocked into the backseat, sacks in hand. Once the door clapped shut, he released the brake and stomped on the gas. 'The Kid,' new to the gang, pointed and shouted, "That a friggin' cop?" Bill didn't take time to verify. He cranked the sedan's wheel hard to the left, and the tires protested loudly, but he didn't care.

Bill sent the sedan down Montclair, barreled through Stanford, leaned into a hard right on another side street, and hit the brake. They piled out of the car and headed towards the black Buick they'd stashed earlier. 'The Kid' fumbled with the Buick's keys in his pocket while Joe and Bill hustled to get the loot from the sedan.

Bill tossed the last sack into the Buick and, before hopping in, remembered something in the trunk of the sedan. He began to double back but decided it wasn't worth the risk. He pivoted and stumbled towards the Buick. Joe leaned forward, gesturing for him to hurry up. Police sirens screeched in the near distance. Bill reached the door and tugged the handle. It was locked. His eyes flared, and he banged on the window, but 'The Kid' stared back blankly and punched the gas, rumbling off and leaving Bill behind with a made car and the law closing in. His only chance was to hoof it! He bolted off at full speed down the block, crossed over properties, and heaved over a sequence of fences, rounding a corner. Bill was on the other side of the neighborhood now, far from the hot car but not far enough, so he kept running past charming houses.

Later, Bill found out that the law was so bent out of shape about the robbery that they dispatched three city department cruisers, called in the Metropolitan District Police armed with tear gas and sub-machine guns, and even called in the Coast Guard. It was as if they had robbed the Federal Reserve and not just some neighborhood bank.

Bill hooked another corner street, crossed through another property, and pushed through laundry lines and neatly trimmed landscaping, emerging onto another block. He slowed his sprint to a brisk stride, wiped his brow with his sleeve, and jammed his hands into his coat pockets. He calmly strolled past a young family but didn't risk a friendly exchange of hellos. Just because he slowed down didn't mean the law had. He had to get out of there. Sirens bled into the neighborhood, and his pulse started jumping again. Bill wound himself up into another exhausting sprint, heaved over a mid-height chain-link fence, and cut into the greenway behind it.

After hoofing it up the hill, he reached the top. Scanning his surroundings, he realized he was on the fairway of a golf club. Nothing but yawning open land stretched out before him, and behind him, mouth-foaming cops were coming up the rear. He must have been somebody's punchline somewhere.

Bill spotted salvation in the near distance and bolted towards it like a Whippet on the racetrack. Reaching the mechanized salvation, he hoisted himself up into the weather-beaten seat and fumbled with the ignition. It gave in and turned over, and he lurched the monstrous, rusty beast into a grating gear.

Suddenly, a young kid, presumably the groundsman, showed up and shouted, "What the hell are you doing there?" over the petrol growl of the motorized mower. Bill searched for an excuse and answered, "There's somebody hurt out there. I've got to go help him!" He pointed indiscriminately to nowhere in particular. The kid followed the point and looked back, "Well, just wait a minute and I'll go with you." The kid dropped a few rocks he was holding and prepared to hop on. Bill grabbed the collar of his overalls and tossed him to the ground, then sat back down and primed the gas pedal, sending the machine into a jerky momentum, slowly building up acceleration.

The groundsman picked himself up, gathered his rocks, and gave chase, thinking he could stop Bill's unusual getaway. Just as Bill crossed over a slope, he heard gunshots. A bullet pinged off the back of the mower. Looking behind, he saw squad cars pouring down the fairway. One of the cars had a maniac hanging out of the back window, taking shots. Then, a horn cut through the gunfire and sirens. Bill spun his head around to see a station wagon driving up the narrow pathway towards him. He cranked the mower's wheel as hard as he could, throwing all of his weight into it, but it was too late, and the machine took a bite out of the front fender of the station wagon. The mower bounced off it, and the shock of the impact made him lose control. Meanwhile, two more shots fired off, and a fourth stung him in the back. Bill twisted, trying to maintain his hold on the driver's seat of the mower, and a sixth shot hit him cold.

Falling off the mower, Bill smashed into the plush turf, bleeding out and clenching grass, writhing in a pain he'd once before known. His insides boiled as if a campfire were crackling within. Then, an eerie moment of pause and silence blanketed the chaos, followed by a distant foghorn of squad car sirens.

The sound of the County District Attorney barging into a room filled Bill's ears. He was angry, not just because of the robbery, but because it had taken place in the exact same building as his office while he was sitting at his desk. The optics of a bank robbery happening right under his nose didn't sit well with him.

Meanwhile, as the D.A. cursed every cop around the hospital bed, Bill lay up in bed with intravenous lines, gauze, and his wrist secured to the bed. The D.A. looked down his pointed nose at Bill, "What's your name?" he asked. Bill didn't give him the benefit of knowing his name. The D.A.'s patience simmered at Bill's refusal to answer. In fact, the only thing Bill gave him was more defiance as he pushed harder and harder for satisfaction.

The D.A. spotted Bill's wedding band, and a sparkle of hope glinted in his eye, bringing a smile to his slim face. "Don't suppose you want her to hear about your escapade…" Bill said laconically, "No one cares where I am." The D.A. sucked his teeth, nodded, and stepped back. He looked at a decorated cop, "We've got nothing on him? First name, nickname? Hell, no initials?" The cop regretfully shook his head, "No sir, nothing. There aren't even any clothing labels or laundry marks."

"Jesus, there's gotta be something. The guy isn't a friggin' ghost!" He looked back at Bill, "…At least not yet," then back at the cop.

"The only thing in his pockets was a few .45 shells, car keys, and about fifty-five bucks."

The D.A. looked back at Bill and chewed on his cheek. "Car keys," he murmured. Just then, two nurses entered the room. "Gentlemen, you'll have to excuse us. This patient has to go to the operating table," and they proceeded to cart Bill out.

Later, Bill was carted back to his guarded room, back to his IVs and heart monitoring electrodes. He lay silently as the two nurses plugged him back in, and his wrist returned to the manacle at the hospital bed. The stitches still burned, and there was an unfamiliar push on his intestine. It had been one hell of a day. He had clopped right up to death's door and given it a rap. Today, he was closer to the grave than he had been during his meritorious tour in the European Theater. Despite everything, he was still here. He let that notion comfort him as he swallowed hard at the sight of two approaching men. The taste was medical and sterile.

"He gonna live through this?" one of the men asked the exiting nurse. She looked back at Bill, paused, and said, "Well, he's off the danger list... But that could change," and left. The taller of the two removed his hat, "You could make this easy on yourself, you know." The smaller one stepped forward and leaned on the door frame, "...he's right." Bill didn't want to make anything easy for any lawman or person he didn't know. But he was also all hopped up on drugs, and just as he began to say his name, a guy popped his thumb-like face into the room and handed the tall guy a slip of paper. The pair looked at it, and their granite faces lit up.

The tall one drummed up the drama, licked his thin lips, and said, "That was a pretty clean caper this morning, wasn't it?"

"I wouldn't say that," Bill muttered.

"Well, I mean, the cops were on-site within four or seven

minutes, right? We had the whole city cinched up, roads blocked, canvases spread out over ten square miles of fields, swamps, and neighborhoods, right? You know there were hundreds dispatched looking for you and your crew, right?"

"You know, Frank," the short one cut in, "they even had the National Guard and copters in the sky, too!"

"Right, right..." the tall one responded. "All that fuss, and your friends, with only small minutes of a head start, managed to elude that cordon of law stomping around. How do you suppose that happens... Bill?"

Hearing his name leaving that idiot's mouth pulled Bill out of the medical fog he was in, like a parachute ripcord. The tall one smiled broadly,

"The car keys you had fit perfectly with some boiler you left off Stanford. Guess what we found in the trunk."

A single leaf of paper tumbled down from his hand onto Bill's chest. He didn't need to look at it. He knew what it was...

"Bill," the tall one said, "...what kind of man pulls a robbery the same day as his own mother's funeral?"

The smaller guy added, "better tell someone you ain't going to make it..."

7

The Pulp Writer

The story "Wings of Hate" was published in *Dare-Devil Aces*, Volume 17, Issue 1, in August 1937. It was written by John N. Makris and is his first published work. Years later, during an interview for a puff piece, Makris told his pal Paul Kneeland at the *Boston Globe* that he was only 16 when the story was sold and published, and as a result, he dropped out of high school. In reality, he was 21.

Despite the embellishment, the pulp writer wasted no time transitioning to true crime in 1937. He jokingly mentioned that he switched because real crime cases' pay better.' Makris further emphasized his wry outlook on financial gain by boldly proclaiming on his letterhead in 1940, 'Crime <u>Does</u> Pay!'—a playful yet pointed testament to the lucrative world of true crime writing.

Makris attributed most of his earnest success to his relentless work ethic, contrasting himself with what he perceived as the laziness of other writers. His ambition and "specialty" in writing about forgotten murders earned him a role in editing and contributing to *Boston Murders*, published in 1948, a collection of dated crimes. As part of the *Regional Murder* series, which detailed old and forgotten crime stories across the country, Makris's contributions included *"Who Killed Fantasia?: The Joseph Fantasia Case"* and *"The Bickford Case."*

Makris allegedly did a stint or two as a background man for defense attorneys Arthur N. Illman and Edward Viola in the slayings of Robert "Tex" Williams, killed over a dispute about a split of proceeds from a New Hampshire robbery, and Mary Saunders, known as the victim of the Dracut "Locket Murder Mystery."

He wrote for *Inside Detective, Crime Detective, Headquarters Detective,* and the *Saturday Evening Post,* among others, allegedly hammering out his tales between 7 a.m. and 9 p.m., amassing about 500 stories over ten years. He tackled articles on notorious robbers such as Jerome Polanski, aka Jerry the Pole, and the Back Bay's Lone Wolf, a criminal folklore within the back alleys of Boston. Due to his perceived tenacity, he also claimed to have solid leads on more than 300 unsolved killings in Massachusetts proper, and nearly 50 for Boston alone.

In 1952, Makris worked as a research man for various cop television programs, notably *Police Story,* a teleplay program. The specific episode Makris researched was entitled *"The Springfield Mass Story,"* aired on May 16th, 1952, an adaptation of the 1935 arsonist case where the bandits would set fires to rob neighboring homes. It was scripted by Max Ehrlich.

In July 1953, Makris returned to the pulps and published a paperback called Nightshade, a hard-boiled prose set on the West Coast with a dip in Tia Juana for "color." Makris said that the story was based on a famous California case but, in fact, was just based on the criminal atmosphere of the time. Later, he told a peer he was working on three crime books, insinuating that paperback originals yielded better advances. There again, Makris was chasing the paycheck.

While toiling away as a freelancer with puff pieces, such as "*60 Million Neckties Will be Bought for Christmas Gifts*," and tawdry book reviews, the writer craved a hit desperately. Then, in 1955 came along Matt Cvetic, an FBI man who went undercover as a 'communist.' Several profiles were written about Mr. Cvetic in the Saturday Evening Post and later were adapted into his 1951 book, *I Was a Communist for the FBI*, which became a mixed bag of success for Cvetic. Later, *The Big Decision: The Story of Matt Cvetic, Counterspy*, according to FBI sources, was written by 'rewrite man' John N. Makris, with Micheal Angelo Musmanno and William Lynch as 'grammarians.'

However, Makris' big break came in the form of the 'first exposé' of the United States Postal Inspection Service, *The Silent Investigators*. Originally entitled: *Postal Inspector* and later, *Guardians of the Mails: The Great Untold Story of the United States Postal Inspection Service*, it was a 526-page manuscript in which the writer earned a handsome advance. Despite the initial promise, the book was published in one printing, with 5,000 copies, and received sluggish sales.

Foreseeing this, Makris took the rights to his book and used newspaper pals turned screenwriters, securing a deal with 20th Century Fox in 1960 to option the book initially as a film but figured it might fair better as a television program, so in May of that year, the show began pre-production with former *I Love Lucy* producer Irving Asher at the helm. Makris was granted an associate producer title. In television, an associate producer assists in various production duties such as research, scriptwriting, and coordination among different departments. This role often helps ensure the smooth operation of production but does not typically involve final decision-making authority.

However, Asher left the project, and the show went into the hands of actor-turned-producer Charles Russell, where a pilot script was written by Jerry Sohl. However, the project went belly up when Russell took off after the success of another program he was involved with called *The Untouchables*.

Sohl reworked the script into a story for the short-lived *The New Breed*, television series giving scripting duties to the in-house husband-wife writer duo Pat and Jesse Lasky, Jr., who had gotten their start in the writing room for *Rescue 8* a year earlier.

Makris soon received a letter from his book's publisher stating that the book, published nearly three years ago, still hadn't sold out. In fact, the three-year-old book had a remaining surplus of stock of 800 books, which Dutton offered to sell to Makris at a discount if he wished. That summer, Makris received another blow: the pilot episode for his dead TV program would be televised in the coming summer, and once again, his name wasn't associated with it.

8

The Appraisal

On Friday, March 16th, 1962, Arthur Tarren, a New Haven Railroad Union Station postal clerk, discovered something unusual. He found a large torn canvas mail sack under a leaking steam valve near the transfer station. Its contents? —close to half a million bucks. Tarren immediately alerted his supervisors, who notified the Chief Postal Inspector Henry B. Montague, kicking off a chain of events that would baffle them and the city.

Montague then dispatched Postal Inspector E.C. Lyons from the Boston Postal Inspector's office to take charge of the investigation. Lyons was a seasoned investigator, familiar with the intricacies of mail theft and fraud.

Lyons' investigation revealed that the canvas bag dispatched on a March 14th Hazardville to Boston shipment was part of a separate shipment that somehow pollinated another shipment en route from Springfield to New York with a pit stop at New Haven. The shipment had contained a total of $541,000, yet only $41,000 was missing. The discovery raised several puzzling questions: How did the bag get to New Haven? And why was only a fraction of the money taken, leaving half a million dollars behind?

The canvas bag housed four smaller pouches, each filled with currency from neighboring banks destined for the Federal Reserve Bank in Boston. The fact that only one pouch was breached suggested that the thief, or thieves, had inside knowledge. They had known where to look but had chosen not to take everything. Lyons theorized that the culprit might have had either enough money or cold feet. The stolen bills were old and tattered, holding little value unless the individual was confident enough that the bills wouldn't crumble into dust or tear or they had access to a bank where the currency would be exchanged for new bills at the Federal Reserve. Since the Federal Reserve insured the money, the loss was more an inconvenience than a financial hit.

Determined to catch the thief, Lyons coordinated with the FBI and the Treasury Service, launching a comprehensive manhunt that spanned Connecticut and stretched to the Canadian border. However, Lyons had a hurdle to deal with. This is due to the usual process of handling, recording, or specifically logging this type of currency. So, it would not be an easy search. Going into stores, businesses, and banks to study their cash intake would yield no results. And the old bills would have reached the Reserve, entered a canvas cart, and tossed into a furnace.

By the next day, postal authorities had labored the area. They questioned the railroad and local post office employees, seeking any information that could lead them to the perpetrators. In addition, the standard $2,000 reward was offered for information leading to a conviction.

Despite these efforts, two days passed, and Lyons still had an incoherent theory. All he could deduce was that the sack had more than likely been taken somewhere between Berlin and New Haven, Connecticut. The unusual nature of the heist, coupled with the incomplete theft, left more questions than answers.

The culprits and the loot are still nowhere to be found.

9

The Bankroll Heist

James Ambrose, the bank custodian, made his way through the Essex Trust Company in West Lynn. For him, March 30th, 1962, was nothing new or unusual. He came in at his usual time, flicked on the lights at his usual time, and went about his custodial routines at his usual time.

After collecting the trash, Ambrose headed towards the back door. As he opened the door, the sound of a quickly approaching vehicle cut through the morning silence. A sedan appeared out of nowhere, backing into the rear parking lot recklessly and slammed into the open door, shocking Ambrose.

A large man with a nylon stocking covering half his face emerged out of the car and drew his pistol on Ambrose.

"Freeze, or I'll blow your head off!" The bandit warned the custodian. Ambrose's heart thumped manically in his chest as the gunman and another entered the building, leaving a third watching Ambrose from the idling sedan.

Customers mill about conducting bank transactions and filling out deposit slips inside the bank. The larger crook firing a shot into the ceiling quickly interrupts the murmur: "This is a stickup; don't anyone move, and no one will get hurt!" The larger bandit swung his gun towards the tellers. "Get back away from those desks," he ordered.

The smaller of the pair of crooks took a crack at leaping over the counter but had a false start. The bandit tried again, landing narrowly on the opposite side and slipping on the linoleum. After getting his feet underneath him, he proceeded to the target. A cart with sacks on it.

"Get the bag!" the large one shouted as he menaced the small crowd with his gun. The smaller one did as commanded, took the bag, lunged it over the same counter, and followed after it. Again, his legs didn't cooperate, so the large one swooped in, helping his partner to his feet.

With their goal achieved, the two crooks went out the same way they came in, and the bank alarm bell rang.

Patrolmen Henry Steadman and Robert Nohelty heard the alarm a few blocks down the road, and their training kicked in. They bolted down to the bank. As they arrived at the back, they just saw a sedan disappearing up the road. Still frozen in fear, Ambrose indicated in the sedan's direction.

The new squad car's wheels screamed in protest as the car's engine forced them into pursuit, speeding down Western Avenue. As they reached the corner, a bystander pointed the officers in the right direction as the robbers' car toed through the streets of Lynn.

Now in hot pursuit, the squad car quickly closed the gap, then gunfire erupted, and the police car was showered with bullets. The gunfire was wild, ricocheting off buildings, doorjambs, and parked vehicles.

Steadman's focus on the pursuit was shattered by the searing bite of a bullet into the flesh of his shoulder. Undeterred, the officers continued the chase and fired back tactfully, swerving through traffic and dodging pedestrians. The pursuit came up Lincoln and Drew with the bumper of the police car just a breath away from the bandits'. Almost as a split-second thought, the bandit's vehicle immediately switched the direction of its turn and went the opposite way, gaining mileage from the unexpected act. Shortly, Steadman and Nohelty came across the bullet-ridden sedan at High and Ferry Streets in Everett.

Meanwhile, a laundry truck lumbered down Ferry Street, Everett, driven by Thomas McBride Jr. then took a turn onto Summer Street to perform his task, and when he returned to the truck to head to the next stop, a man with a gun appeared before the laundry truck and ordered McBride to get into the back of the truck, or he'd blow McBride's head off. Two other masked gunmen piled into the truck. McBride was thrown into the back, a towel thrown over his head, and ordered to keep down.

The truck then made a handful of stops for the other crooks to get off the truck and disappear.

A final stop came at Roxbury.

Meanwhile, back at the victim bank detectives were able to pull off a fingerprint from the teller's counter that the smaller crook bounded over. Given the meager description of the bandits and the methodology, the detectives theorized that this may have been the work of Albert "Bumpy" Nussbaum, the 'brains' and Bobby "One-Eye" Wilcoxson, the 'brawn' of the Bumpy Gang, currently the FBI's number one wanted men for a bank robbery that resulted in the death of an officer. There had been soft-bellied reports that the gang had been spotted recently in the area.

The following day, at 2:30 a.m., a telephone call came into the Lynn Police Department. A woman on the other line told the desk sergeant, "If you are interested in the money taken from the Essex Bank in Lynn, go to the rooming house on Temple Street, Boston. It is all there. I've seen it myself."

Quickly, the Division 3 squad of the Lynn police department sprang into action under the lead of Lieutenant-Inspector Edward Ray and Sergeant Charles Starkey. The officers smashed into the rooming house and turned it over, looking for the $28,500 that had been stolen from the bank. In the brownstone, officers found 15 individuals. 13 of them were elderly and infirm. Two were under the age of 45. They were questioned intensely but were cut loose after having an airtight alibi.

Shortly the same day at 5:30, Robert Kane, owner and operator of Kane's Donut Shop at the corner of Lincoln Ave and Dudley Street, Saugus, discovered a curious-looking car had been parked there. In fact, that car had been there since the day before. Kane called it in to get towed away.

When a police officer appeared in response to the call, he looked over the car to see if anything could identify its owner. Inside the vehicle, two women's wigs, two Halloween masks, an army weather jacket, two army jackets, and a kerchief were found. The officer called it in, and it was clear that this car had been an intended getaway car that had to be abandoned during the close chase.

Upon further inspection, the car had been stolen from a lot in Lynn on December 5th, 1961. While the car was impounded at the State Police barracks, it was discovered that the license plate had been masterfully tampered with and was nearly missed. The plates had four numbers on them, and two of those numbers were changed from "59," indicating the registration year, to "61," implying that the vehicle's registration had not expired.

Without any solid leads, Chief of Detectives John H. Linehan called for a late afternoon meeting on April 3rd with FBI, State Detectives, and District Attorney John P.S. Burke at the Lynn Police Department to exchange information that each agency had relating to the first bank robbery of the city. Their collective report was discussed later at the April 11th Essex County Investigators' Association at the Willey House in Swampscott. A monthly association, with Charles Witham, Lynn's Police Identification expert, as its president and Detective W.J. Carlin of the Swampscott police department as its secretary, discusses mutual hang-ups of crime prevention and law enforcement. There State Police Lieutenant Andrew J. Tuney presented the report.

Despite the communal discussions about the case, the single fingerprint, and the abandoned getaway car, all leads about the bank robbery fizzled out and laid dormant for five months.

The hacky bank robbers remained at large.

10

Truck Number 142984

He drained the mug of the remaining black liquid, pulled two singles out of his pocket, and put them on the counter. He stood up, folded his newspaper under his arm, waved goodbye to the familiar waitress, and started down the block.

It's August, early afternoon, and the day had been just another ordinary Tuesday for Patrick Schena, 35, cleanly put together and a 12-year veteran of the United States Post Office, Boston. He hooked a corner, walked along, and entered the Postal Annex building. He picked up his familiar assignment, a petrol credit card, strolled to the garage, and signed out a red, white, and blue three-quarter-ton Dodge Mail truck, Number 142984. It's 2:45 pm. He hears the tired instructions to fill in Hyannis before making the first pick-up. He smiles, nods, takes the keys, glances over the vehicle, and climbs into its barren cab.

There is no two-way radio or other concealed security equipment inside. Beside the driver's seat is a simple folding chair bolted to the floor of the cab for the guard. The motor growled awake at the ignition key's insistence, and the machine lurched forward out of its parking space and was directed toward its first stop on the itinerary.

Schena swung the truck into the garage at the main post office in Boston. William Barrett, 55, a long-time employee, mainly in the sorting department, stood up and introduced himself to Schena as the replacement guard for Schena's usual co-pilot, William Gullette, who had just started his two-week vacation yesterday. The pair walked to the cage, signed for their .45 pistols, and departed for Cape Cod.

On the way down, Barrett and Schena became acquainted and reminisced about their first meeting some weeks back at the Deer Island firing range for training. Barrett confessed to Schena that he had never stepped foot on the Cape in his 51 years in Massachusetts. The conversation then turned to current events and the collective mourning of the sparkling specter that is Marilyn.

The truck pulled into the Esso Gas Station in Hyannis, refueled, and arrived at the Hyannis Post Office. The pair parked the truck in the lot, locked the doors, and walked into the post office carrying a zippered bag that held their revolvers. Barrett handed the bag to the registry clerk. The cargo was still being prepared, so Schena and Barrett grabbed dinner across the street.

After their meal, they went back. Schena hopped into the truck and prepared it for loading. Barrett looked over the manifest that listed the registered currency pouches impending in Boston. With the truck now backed into the loading dock, the pouches were loaded, each bag making a soft metallic thud as it dropped to the trailer floor. Bill Tinney, the registry clerk, scribbled down the truck number and watched the truck disappear from the parking lot. Bill ambled back into the building, picked up the telephone receiver, told the party on the other end, "It just left," and hung it back up. It's 6:30 pm.

Schena traced the route back and sailed over the Sagamore Bridge. He hooked a right and rolled into the Buzzards Bay Post Office parking lot. Another mail truck was docked, so the pair sat and waited. Once the other truck departed, Barrett hopped out of his seat and went inside while Schena readied the truck for the second pick-up. Inside, Barrett chatted with Ronald Haskell, the Buzzards Bay registry clerk. Shortly after, a canvas cart was pushed out, and the truck was loaded again with several additional registered pouches containing currency. Barrett signed off on the document, the seven bags were packed, and the double locking doors were secured. Then the pair made their way along the north bank of the Cape Cod Canal and to the Sagamore Circle; Schena switched on the dimmers and the truck's body lights, then headed northbound to Boston via Route 3, a limited access divided highway into the fading dusk.

The truck lumbered through as a summer's mist began. Schena trekked seven miles of asphalt when two cars flashed beside them, "Jesus," Barrett shouted, "They must be going eighty," Schena stated, and the pair watched the tail lights drop under the horizon. Further up the road, Barrett points out that the two speeding cars are now parked by the Clark Road exit on the right shoulder. Both drivers were bent over, examining or tinkering with the front license plate; one of the drivers stared back at the truck as it passed by. Barrett suggested that one must have busted up the other during their race.

The truck drove through the overpass, and when it did, two other cars exploded past the mail truck. Something seemed strange but not strange enough to become overly concerned.

The truck continued five more miles at the typical highway speed of 45 miles per hour, and the southbound lane became blotted out by tree branches, leaves, and grassy cliffs. Barrett leaned forward towards the windshield, wincing out of it. Schena clutched the wheel tighter. Up ahead, the two other speeding cars were partially parked on the shoulder, similar to the others. A policeman stepped out into the road and raised his white-gloved hand.

Schena brought the truck to a halt to avoid hitting the officer. Just as he did, a car leaped from the right side of the road behind the officer, taking up both lanes of the highway; behind the truck, the second car swung around, blocking any attempt at reversal. "Sonovabitch" Barrett uttered as he braced himself. The driver of the vehicle ahead of them burst out from behind the car door, armed with a shotgun, and advanced on the truck's left side. Another man ran up from the darkness to the truck's passenger side. Both Schena and Barrett were covered by gun barrels as the officer stood supervising in the headlights. The men with guns barked at the driver and guard of the mail truck, demanding that the doors be opened.

Schena and Barrett, dazzled at the sight, reacted slowly only to be aggressively encouraged by the thrusting gun barrels and threats of heads being blown clean off. One of the men had on a police cap, and he called out to the officer in the headlights, "Tony, let's get on with it." Tony approached the truck. "Get the gate open, Buster," Tony replied. Buster commanded Schena to open the sliding door to the cargo compartment. Schena pulled the keys from the ignition and unlocked the cage. Buster reached over with one hand, pulled the door open, and gestured for the pair to get into the back.

They were told to lie down on the floor. Schena dropped

to his stomach and folded his forearm underneath his face. He was then poked in the back with the barrel of a shotgun. The voice behind the barrel commanded Schena to put both wrists behind his back. Barrett was also commanded to lie down. Once these orders were followed, the blocking car in the front pulled back, corrected its angle, and drove forward. Meanwhile, Buster got situated behind the wheel of the mail truck, and Tony got comfortable in the bolted chair, and the hulking vehicle followed the Oldsmobile northerly.

For five tense minutes, the drive was quiet except for the sound of the grumbling motor and jostling suspension. The truck hooked a hard right without warning, and the road became coarse and potted. Tony stood sea-legged and attended to applying bonds to the ankles of Schena and Barrett from a concoction of clothesline and Rexall Adhesive tape.

The harrowing ride continued for an estimated 20 additional minutes before it came to a stop. The cab-passenger-side door opened, and Tony lugged the mail bags out from under Schena and Barrett. Whispered words of urgency were heard, but no faces or any sense of location could be observed. "See you in Providence, Tony." Someone said, "No names, god damnit," someone else said, cutting into the sentence. One by one, the mail sacks left the truck's cargo compartment,"Get the big one," someone ordered. With the big one removed, six sacks were left in the truck. The cab door clapped shut, and the idling motor pressed on.

After a few more moments on the road, Tony got up and returned to the truck's cargo hold. Tony knelt, took hold of Schena's writs, and bound them together. Then he took Barrett's wrists and bound them up tighter in front of him.

Schena's wrists behind his back were bound to Barrett's wrists with another length or two of Rexall adhesive tape. After this, Tony dragged the remaining five bags towards the cab.

The road began to smooth again, and then the truck stopped. The hijackers remained in the cab for a few moments, controlling their adrenaline and labored breathing. The driver leaped from the cab, leaving the door open. The sound of someone turning in their seat then, "Stay down," the voice said, "for ten minutes," then crawled out of the cab, not using the passenger side. Schena slowly lifted his cheek up from the floor and opened his eyes. The cab was empty, and only a broken shaft of yellow street light poured through the windshield. Schena shuffled to get a better bearing of the stop. The muzzle of a shotgun quickly appeared after the passenger side door wrenched open, "Get down, goddamnit, or I'll blow your head off!" A voice roared, pinging against the aluminum and steel inside the truck. Schena quickly complied and squeezed his eyes tightly, preparing for oblivion.

A kaleidoscope of dark purple and sparking blue electric stars brightened through the soupy blackness. An engine mumbles coarsely in the middle distance. A heavy clapping *thunk* cuts through. An axle shifts, sand and gravel give way unwillingly to rolling pressure.

Patrick Schena opens his eyes.

The truck shudders from passing traffic. He works his bindings loose and frees his wrists, then frees Barrett's. Schena shuffles to the cab. The passenger side door is still open, so he waits. Still nothing. He spills out from the cab with ankles still bound together. He hobbles around the engine to survey the landscape.

Now our story begins…

www.ingramcontent.com/pod-product-compliance
Lightning Source LLC
Chambersburg PA
CBHW030505130626
46549CB00007B/2860